# THE PROPHETS

# INTERPRETING BIBLICAL TEXTS

INTERPRETING **ibt** BIBLICAL TEXTS

# The Prophets

# James M. Ward

## LLOYD R. BAILEY, SR.
### and
## VICTOR P. FURNISH, EDITORS

ABINGDON PRESS      NASHVILLE

## THE PROPHETS

**Library of Congress Cataloging in Publication Data**

WARD, JAMES MERRILL, 1928-
  The Prophets.
  (Interpreting Biblical texts)
  Bibliography: p.
  1. Bible. O.T. Prophets—Criticism, interpretation, etc. 2. Prophets.
  I. Title. II. Series.
  BS1505.2.W37      224'.06      81-20575      AACR2

**ISBN 0-687-34370-4** (pbk.)

MANUFACTURED BY THE PARTHENON PRESS AT
NASHVILLE, TENNESSEE, UNITED STATES OF AMERICA

# INTERPRETING BIBLICAL TEXTS:
## Editors' Foreword

The volumes in this series have been planned for those who are convinced that the Bible has a meaning for our life today, and who wish to enhance their skills as interpreters of the biblical texts. Such interpreters must necessarily engage themselves in two closely related tasks: (1) determining as much as possible about the original meaning of the various biblical writings, and (2) determining in what respect these texts are still meaningful today. The objective of the present series is to keep both of these tasks carefully in view, and to provide assistance in relating the one to the other.

Because of this overall objective it would be wrong to regard the individual volumes in this series as commentaries, as homiletical expositions of selected texts, or as abstract discussions of "the hermeneutical problem." Rather, they have been written in order to identify and illustrate what is involved in relating the meaning of the biblical texts in their own times and places to their meaning in ours. Biblical commentaries and other technical reference works sometimes focus exclusively on the first, paying little or no attention to the second. On the other hand, many attempts to expound the contemporary "relevance" of biblical themes or passages pay scant attention to the intentions of the texts themselves. And although one of the standard topics of "hermeneutics" is how a text's original meaning relates to its present meaning, such discussions often employ highly technical philosophical language and proceed with little reference to concrete examples. By way of contrast, the present volumes are written in language that will be understood by scholars, clergy and laypersons alike, and they deal with concrete texts, actual problems of interpretation, and practical procedures for moving from "then" to "now."

Each contributor to this series is committed to three basic tasks: (1) a description of the salient features of the particular type of biblical literature or section of the canon assigned; (2) the identification and explanation of the basic assumptions that guide the analysis and explication of those materials; and (3) the discussion of possible contemporary meanings of representative texts, in view of the specified assumptions with which the interpreter approaches them. Considerations that should be borne in mind by the interpreter in reflecting upon contemporary meanings of these texts are introduced by the sign ● and are accentuated with a different size of type.

The assumptions which are brought to biblical interpretation may vary from one author to the next, and will undoubtedly vary from those of many readers. Nonetheless, we believe that the present series, by illustrating how careful interpreters carry out their tasks, will encourage readers to be more reflective about the way they interpret the Bible.

Lloyd R. Bailey, Sr.
Duke Divinity School

Victor Paul Furnish
Perkins School of Theology
Southern Methodist University

# CONTENTS

# I. INTRODUCTION

Our subject is the Prophets: the books of Isaiah, Jeremiah, Ezekiel, and the Twelve (Minor) Prophets. The task of interpreting these books is fascinating and important. It is also formidable. It is important because of the central place occupied by the Prophets in the canon of the Bible and in Christian proclamation. It is formidable because of the size and complexity of the books themselves. The fascination in working with the books of the prophets is due to the rhetorical variety and power of their oracles and the intensity of their engagement with their people and with God.

The Prophets constitute fully one-fourth of the OT. Their length alone makes it difficult to provide a guide to their interpretation in one brief book. Moreover, the difficulty is compounded by the diversity of the material and the absence of explicit aids to understanding in the text itself. In spite of the superficial appearance of rational order and continuity in parts of the prophetic corpus, much of it is a loose, even haphazard, arrangement of oracles, laments, visions, sayings, narratives, prayers, and other kinds of writing. The shape and extent of the literary units vary greatly and are often difficult to determine.

Indications of date, historical setting, audience, and purpose are infrequent, and the authorship of many sections is unknown.

Nevertheless, the Prophets command our attention. Quite apart from the intrinsic literary merits of the prophetic books, which are sufficient to justify the attention of modern readers, their theological importance requires the attention of responsible ministers and students of the Bible. The books of the prophets are more explicit theologically than other parts of the OT, so they lend themselves more directly to religious discourse. Furthermore, the dominant forms of prophetic speech are closer to those of the modern preacher than most of the rest of the Bible is. The oracles of the ancient prophets can serve to some extent as models for preaching, and they provide a rich resource of thematic material for this purpose.

The writings of the Bible are not uniformly authoritative for the Christian witness of faith, and they have not been employed equally in the life of the church. Among the writings of the OT, the Prophets have occupied a place of special regard. This was true already in the earliest church, and it has continued to be true down to the present time. The Prophets are quoted and alluded to hundreds of times in the NT. Of the other OT books, only the Psalms, Genesis, Exodus, and Deuteronomy show comparable usage. The primary focus of the NT writers' interest in the Prophets is in the messianic prophecies, but there are many other elements of the prophetic message that informed their understanding and influenced their proclamation. They cited the messianic prophecies because they believed them to be fulfilled in Jesus' life, death, and resurrection. They cited other passages from the Prophets for a variety of reasons, but all of these rooted in the conviction that God had spoken through the prophets and that this word was as true and lively for them as for the first hearers. God's word was rich and varied, but what it communicated most of all was the knowledge of God and of God's relationship with people. The Scriptures were addressed to them, and in the Scriptures, especially in the Pentateuch and the Prophets, they found the disclosure of God's love, God's righteousness, God's purpose for humanity, the faith and obedience God required, the meaning of life and suffering and death, the characteristics of the true family of God, and the identity of God's Messiah.

A well-informed, intellectually open modern reader cannot read the Bible as the word of God as directly and simply as the early church did. We know things about the Bible and ask questions about it that earlier Christians and Jews did not know or think to ask. The expansion of knowledge about ancient literature, history, and religion that has occurred since the Enlightenment has led to an understanding of the origin and development of the biblical writings, and of the communities that produced them, which calls into question the naive conviction that God speaks to us directly and consistently in the Bible. We are only too aware of the inconsistencies in the biblical witness, the intellectual and cultural limitations of the biblical writers, and the fragmentary and disjointed character of the surviving biblical documents. It is impossible for us today to see the word of God simply, fully, and uniformly in every page of the Bible. If we wish to find the word of God there, we must seek it within, through, and behind the words of the Bible and not merely in them.

Not all students of the Bible are interested in finding the word of God in, or through, the Bible. Some are interested in it primarily for esthetic or historical reasons. For example, one of my fellow students in graduate school wrote his M.A. thesis on the militia in the OT, in order to learn whether it might serve as a model for modern Israeli military science. He was an atheist and had no interest whatever in the Bible as the word of God.

The purpose of this present book is to seek the word of God in the writings of the prophets. More specifically, it is to reflect upon the principles, assumptions, and convictions that are operating in my mind as I try to interpret prophetic writings as bearers of the word of God for me. It is hoped that by observing this, readers will be helped to reflect more adequately upon the underlying principles and convictions that govern their own reading of the Prophets and control their efforts to interpret these writings in the midst of contemporary religious communities. We will not do this reflecting abstractly, but in the act of interpreting particular biblical texts. The principles of interpretation are not to be learned in advance and then applied to specific texts. They are to be learned—and revised—in the very process of studying specific texts. More usually, they are not made explicit in the act of interpreting, nor is the interpreter always conscious of them.

Our task, then, is twofold. It is to interpret selected prophetic texts in order to see whether and to what extent we may discern the word of God in them, and to examine the assumptions and convictions that affect the way we deal with these texts and the conclusions we reach in interpreting them.

If examining methods and presuppositions were the sole aim of this book, it would not matter which texts we selected from the corpus assigned to us, so long as we chose ones that provided ample opportunity to exhibit our methods and presuppositions. This is not our sole aim, however. We wish also to interpret texts that contain prominent themes of the books of the prophets. It is important, not only to know *how* to interpret the words of the prophets and to recognize what we are doing when we engage in this interpretation, but also to know *what* the prophets were most concerned to say and what this message might mean to us.

We will not examine *all* the principles, assumptions, and convictions that underlie and control our interpretation of the chosen texts. For one thing, we may fail to recognize some of them, at least some of the time. A few may remain unconscious, even in the face of our best efforts to become self-conscious about them. For another thing, some may be too trivial or too obvious to warrant discussion. Others may be recurrent in our working but not require repetition in our discussion. For these and other reasons, including limitations of space, our treatment of assumptions will not be exhaustive in every section of the exposition. However, we hope it may be full enough to serve the stated purpose of this series.

Similarly, our exposition of the themes of the prophetic message must be selective also. Here, the limitation of space is decisive. Nevertheless, we shall try to give a fair representation of the major themes of the Prophets, using texts that have been especially important in Christian usage through the ages. Many of these texts are contained in the Ecumenical Lectionary, so widely used today in Christian worship and study.

The exposition is organized into four chapters. In the first we will consider texts relating to the call, commission, and ministry of Isaiah, Amos, Jeremiah, Ezekiel, and the Servant of Yahweh (in Isaiah 40–55). In addition to discussing the theological implications of these texts generally, we will ponder their possible bearing on an understanding of ministry today.

In the next chapter we will deal with the theme of worship and idolatry. Jeremiah, Hosea, Ezekiel, and Second Isaiah will provide the major texts. The formal worship of God in the sanctuary will figure in the discussion, but worship in a broader sense will be considered also.

In chap. 4 we will turn to the righteousness of God. Most of the contents of the books of the prophets could be discussed under this heading. The issues raised or implied by the selected texts include the justice of God, God's covenant with Israel, the day of wrath, punishment and forgiveness, individual responsibility and the righteousness of God, God and the foreign nations, providence and history, the prosperity of the wicked, and the new covenant. The texts come mainly from Isaiah, Jeremiah, and Ezekiel.

Finally, we will take up the theme of God and the gods. God is the subject of everything considered in the other chapters, so one may wonder what remains to be said in a separate chapter on this topic. The aim will be, not to repeat or summarize what is said in the preceding discussion, but to interpret two specific texts in which the identity of God is the explicit focus of concern. These texts are Isaiah 40 and Ezekiel 34.

## Some Basic Assumptions About Nature and History

I have several principles—basic convictions—that should be made clear at the outset, because they affect everything I do in biblical interpretation. Indeed, I believe they are essential to any effort to appropriate the message of the Bible in our own lives.

The first of these convictions is that nature, both in its human and nonhuman aspects, is essentially the same today as it was in biblical times. The face of our planet has changed somewhat, a number of animal species have become extinct, and human beings have devised new ways of using and consuming natural resources. Thus, many new things have happened to and upon the earth. However, it is the same earth—the same, basic physical environment, operating in the same ways—that it was three thousand years ago. Human nature is also essentially the same now as it was then. In other words, there has been fundamental continuity for humankind and for its physical environment from biblical times to our own era.

A corollary—and this is our second basic conviction—is that physical events that can happen in nature (human and nonhuman) in one age can happen in another, but those that cannot happen in one cannot happen in another. Thus, if an iron axhead cannot float in water in our time, one could not have floated in Elisha's time; so the account in 2 Kgs 6:1-7 is a legend.

New things emerge in nature that were not there before, but their emergence results from the same natural processes that have always been at work. Thus, a volcano can appear where none was before, but it will be created by the same processes that produced volcanoes in earlier times.

Historical events are a different matter. Since each individual human being is unique, the interactions of human beings are infinite in their variety. What emerges from these interactions is a constantly changing aggregation of institutions, associations, happenings, movements, and communications. And all of this is unpredictable and uncontrollable. Nevertheless, the kinds of interaction among human beings, and the psychological concomitants of these interactions, are similar today to what they were in biblical times. Our material culture and our technology have changed drastically in three thousand years, but people are essentially the same today as they were in ancient Israel.

The third basic assumption—and it is closely related to the others—is that human beings are related to God in the same way today as in biblical times. The language used to describe this relationship may change, but the relationship itself is the same. In itself it is not static, but dynamic and multifaceted—a living, personal relationship. However, what the biblical writers experienced in relation to God we may experience also, and what we experience many of them experienced. Not all of us have the same experiences they had, but anything they experienced we may experience also. Conversely, anything we experience they might have experienced, too.

If these assumptions are not correct, then I do not see how we can make any sense of the Bible for ourselves. If human existence in the biblical world were essentially different from ours, and if God interacted with people differently in that time, then we could not know what their existence was, and we could not share their knowledge of God. In that case we could not appropriate what they said about God in any relevant or effective way.

## The Authority of the Old Testament

The Bible is an indispensable source of the knowledge of God. The understanding of God expressed in it is decisive for Christian faith. The witness of faith in the OT is decisive for Jewish faith also, but it would be presumptuous of me to speak about this. Jews and Christians have much in common in their religious and moral understanding. There is little difference between the Jewish and Christian expositions of the OT that I have read over the years. The laws of the Pentateuch are still authoritative for conservative Jews, but Christian interpreters do not uniformly share that conviction. On the other hand, Christians believe Jesus of Nazareth to be the Messiah promised in the OT, and Jews do not share that conviction. Otherwise, it is difficult to distinguish Christian from Jewish exegesis of the OT. There is much variety among Jewish works, as there is among Christian, but the differences cut across the two traditions rather than following them. There are fundamentalist scholars on both sides and historically critical scholars on both sides. Fundamentalist interpretations sound much alike whether they are Jewish or Christian and so do historically critical interpretations. Seldom can one tell whether a work is written by a Jew or a Christian merely from what is said about the OT. Therefore, I would be surprised if there were much written here that would be unacceptable to Jewish readers solely because of incompatibility with Jewish faith. As a Christian I believe the norm for faith to be the NT witness of faith in Jesus Christ. For me this is the ultimate standard of truth about God and about the meaning and goal of human life. However, the NT witness presupposes the OT witness. Most of the categories of NT thought are drawn from the OT, so the NT would be incomprehensible without it. Therefore, Christians and Jews hold much more in common in their understanding of the OT than they hold separately.

The biblical witness of faith in God is decisive for my faith. Any profession of the knowledge of God, unsupported by the central witness of the Bible, is, I believe, untrue. The Bible is indispensable for Christian understanding; however, the biblical witness is not uniform in all its parts. Convictions stated in one place are sometimes contrary to those expressed elsewhere. The Bible is not only the vehicle of the word of God. It is also the record of Israel's experience. Israel learned much about God during the course of her history and was forced to unlearn much as well. Part of the story of this development is contained in the OT. Clearly, our responsibility is to read the story as an account of changing perceptions of God and not as a uniform, unchanging witness that is binding for us.

Some readers of the Bible regard it as the infallible word of God, accurate and true in all its parts and on every level of meaning. This view is often called the literal view of the Bible. However, I prefer not to use the term in this way. The opposite to "literal" is "figurative," or "allegorical." The whole thrust of modern biblical scholarship is to understand and interpret the Bible literally, that is, to ascertain the meaning of the words in the way they were intended by the writers. The alternative to this is to reinterpret them figuratively, allegorically, or "spiritually." The latter is a highly subjective endeavor, widespread in previous eras, but largely rejected by scholars of all faiths since the Reformation. What we should ascertain now is the literal meaning of the words. Whether we regard the literal sense as the word of God is another matter.

The so-called literalist view of the Bible identifies the word of God with *all* the words of the biblical text. Thus, it regards all the words as authoritative for faith. The assumption underlying this view is that unless everything the Bible says is true, nothing can be trusted. If one doubts the accuracy or truth of anything in the text, where does the doubting stop? If anything is questionable, isn't everything questionable?

The answer to this question is yes. Everything *is* questionable. That is to say, every individual statement made in the Bible is subject to examination in the light of the total biblical witness of faith, the experience of the community of believers through the centuries, accumulated human knowledge, and our own reason and experience. When this examination is made, many statements in the Bible are found to be inaccurate or wrong or theologically unacceptable. But the central witness of faith in God is not lost. Indeed, it becomes clearer. The Bible contains reliable testimony to the truth about God, humanity, life, the meaning of history, moral responsibility, and the nature of community, among other things. This witness can be discerned by an earnest seeker. And the discernment will be enhanced, not impeded, by a rigorous scrutiny of the words of the biblical text. What modern scholars call the historical-critical method is not a roadblock to faith in God, but is an aid to such faith. The biblical witness of faith undergirds the kind of fearless criticism involved in the use of this method. Indeed, for me, as for many others, faith in God *requires* this kind of criticism. I do not accept the biblical witness of faith *in spite* of the results of historical-critical study, but, in part, *because* of them. For me, belief in the inerrancy of the Bible is incompatible with the knowledge of God proclaimed in the Bible. Historical criticism of the Bible is not a retreat from faith but a necessary consequence of it. Nothing essential to faith can be lost by it, while much that is unessential, or even detrimental, to faith can be identified by it. I believe it to be an essential means of knowledge, including the knowledge of God. Not all believers need to employ it, or even be aware of it. However, the Christian community as a whole cannot bear true witness without it.

Everything in the Bible is a human statement and reflects, in different ways and varying degrees, the limitations of human understanding and knowledge. There is no single statement in the Bible that can be accepted as true simply because it is contained there—not even statements about God. Everything must be examined and weighed by our reason, in the light of our accumulated knowledge and experience, and in the light of the central biblical witness of faith. None of us can do this adequately alone. It is a shared responsibility, and we fulfill it in continual dialogue with one another.

Biblical statements about the origin and working of our physical environment and our bodies are subject to correction in the light of advancing knowledge. For example, we know that disease is caused by germs and other organic factors, and not by demons or curses; therefore, we must reject many biblical statements in this area. Even if we allow room for a "demonic" element in disease (i.e., psychogenic disorders), there is still much in the Bible about human illness that has to be rejected as wrong.

Again, we know the earth is not flat but spherical, and that it is not circled daily by the sun but rotates on its own axis and orbits around the sun. Therefore, we must correct what the Bible says about these matters. Indeed, in every area of natural science the Bible is subject to correction in the light of accumulated human knowledge and practiced reason.

In the area of history the situation is similar, yet different. The biblical writers' knowledge of history was extremely limited. Their sources were fragmentary and often legendary. They did not have sufficient information available to give a reliable account of the past, and they did not keep sufficient records of current events to provide adequate sources for subsequent writers. Therefore, every historical statement in the Bible is subject to correction in the light of fuller knowledge. The problem here is that we do not have adequate independent sources to do much correcting. Thus, our situation here is very different from that in the physical sciences. Nevertheless, we should adopt the same approach to the Bible in both areas. Because we know how limited and inaccurate the biblical writers' knowledge of science and history was, we cannot accept *any* biblical statement in these areas uncritically. It is not a case of trusting the accuracy and validity of what is said unless there is good reason to reject it. Rather it is a case of *not* accepting anything said unless there is good reason to do so. The Bible is simply not authoritative in matters of science or history. In these realms it is subject to the same standards of criticism that apply to any other writings. Little of biblical science has survived the advancement of knowledge. However, much of biblical history has proved to be usable. The OT is a good source for the history of ancient Israel, but still it must be used critically.

The authority of the Bible for faith lies entirely in the area of faith, that is the knowledge of God. The biblical witness of faith is discernible to anyone who takes the trouble to study the Bible carefully, with an open mind, and with the help of other earnest students, including biblical scholars and theologians. This witness is discernible to anyone. However, there are dimensions of it that require faith in order to be truly understood. The knowledge of God is not purely intellectual, although it involves the intellect completely. It is also experiential; it engages the heart and will as well as the intellect. One cannot fully understand the knowledge of God about which the Bible speaks unless one shares in this knowledge personally, that is, unless one has faith. And the final test of the truth of the biblical witness of faith is faith itself, both in the individual person and in the community of believers.

## Inspiration

The question of the inspiration of the Bible is finally the same as that of its authority. If we ask whether the Bible *itself* is inspired, it is the same thing as asking whether it is authoritative. Is it the word of God? Is it true? All the same issues and considerations are involved whether we are concerned with the Bible's authority or with its inspiration.

To ask whether the *writers* of the Bible were inspired is a different question. However, we find in the end that there are no objective tests of literary inspiration other than the writings themselves; therefore we are forced back where we began, asking whether the biblical writings are inspired. There is no evidence that the processes of perception or communication of the biblical writers were different from those of other people. Their inspiration, to the extent that they were inspired, consisted solely in the content of their communication. We call them inspired because their communications are inspiring (beautiful, true, moving, edifying).

In biblical times dreams and visions were sometimes thought to be better sources of knowledge about God, or the future, than the ordinary waking mind. However, there is considerable doubt about this belief expressed in the Bible, too. And *we* know that the contents of dreams and visions are subject to the same canons of reliability as other forms of information. Truth can be perceived in dreams or visions or in any other mental state. There are many different kinds of truth. Whether a communication is true (or beautiful) cannot be decided on the basis of the mental process that produced it or the mental state in which it was produced. It can only be decided on other grounds. It is the *content* of the communication that determines whether it is true, or "inspired," not the source. Exactly the same thing is true of all communications. An inspired artist or writer or composer is one who produces inspired works of art, literature, or music. There is no way of locating the cause of the inspiration or analyzing the process. The mental processes of the creators are the same as those of other people. Why some produce beautiful or inspiring or edifying works and others do not is a mystery beyond human knowing. It simply happens. But, in any case, to say that a work is inspired is to say that it is true, in whatever way one means this term. In regard to the Bible, to say that its writings are true is to say that they are authoritative for faith. Thus, the inspiration and authority of the Bible are one and the same. The Bible is inspired to the same extent that it is authoritative. How far that is we have already discussed.

## The Books of the Prophets

Literary context does affect the meaning of a text; therefore, we must take account of an entire book or the prophetic books as we try to interpret representative passages within them. The more we know about the origin and purpose of the books, their shape and component parts, the social settings in which they were produced, the better we may understand an individual text. Frequently we can also be helped by studying a text in relation to others of a similar type, in the same book or in other books. Some questions of context and literary relationship will be raised in the course of our treatment of individual texts and do not need to be mentioned here. Others, however, especially those of a more general kind, may be reviewed more appropriately here, before we begin the interpretation of specific texts.

My purpose is not to survey the entire prophetic literature and all the attendant questions of authorship, date, composition, and historical background, as well as the present state of scholarly discussion. Such surveys are readily available in Bible dictionaries, introductions, and commentaries (see the Aids for the Interpreter), and it would be a misuse of space to duplicate them here. However, it seems only fair to the reader to say something about the view of the prophetic books that informs the judgments made in the remainder of this book.

All four of the books of the prophets—Isaiah, Jeremiah, Ezekiel, and The Twelve—are composite works. Each is highly diverse in the kinds of material it contains and in authorship and date of composition. Large portions of these books were composed by anonymous writers. With the exception of Jeremiah, even the writers whose names we know remain effectively anonymous, since we know little or nothing about them as persons. This literary situation is frustrating to us. We would like to know who wrote what parts of these books, what their literary and theological intentions were, who their audience was, and so forth. Only in a few instances does the Bible provide this information.

Two principal responses have been made to this literary situation in the prophetic canon. Some students (scholars) have tried to supply the missing information by subjecting the texts to rigorous literary analysis and drawing inferences from the results. Other readers have denied that a problem exists. This second group of interpreters accepts the biblical statements of authorship as correct. Thus, Isaiah wrote the Book of Isaiah, Jeremiah wrote the Book of Jeremiah, and so forth. This view is held naively by many readers of the Bible who are unaware of critical scholarship. It is held dogmatically by others who are acquainted with critical scholarship but reject it for theological reasons. Believing in the inerrancy of the Bible, they accept the attributions of authorship in the books themselves and find various ways of explaining away any alleged evidence to the contrary. It matters a great deal to them whether the prophetic books were actually written by the men to whom they are attributed. The assumption underlying this view of the Prophets is that the writings would lose their authority if the attributions of authorship were incorrect. We have already commented on this belief above.

Ironically, a similar assumption underlies much critical scholarship. Many scholars who accept the historical-critical method of biblical study have regarded the portions of the prophetic books which can be attributed to the prophets themselves as "authentic" and those which cannot, as "inauthentic." The tacit assumption was that a text had greater worth if the author were known than if it were anonymous. To put it another way, the prophets whose names are given in the Bible were assumed to be better prophets than the writers whose names were not. Fortunately, this assumption has been widely exposed to scrutiny in recent years and rejected by many scholars. Nevertheless, it is so pervasive in the work of earlier generations of scholars that it is difficult to eradicate. It requires conscious effort to resist, especially by those of us who were schooled in it.

The conviction which I hold in this matter, together with many other readers of the Bible, is that the worth of a writing is not determined by who wrote it. The ultimate value of a text is intrinsic. The same thing is true of works of art or musical compositions. A bad painting by a good artist is still a bad painting, though it may have commercial value merely because of the reputation of the painter. A good painting by an unknown artist is no less good because the artist is unknown, and it would be no better if it were found to be by a great artist. In the case of the biblical literature, we need not be anxious to prove who the author of a text was before we can take it seriously as a true and lively word. Great texts are great, whoever wrote them. Each text should be judged on its own merits.

We need not be anxious theologically (or esthetically) over questions of authorship, but we may properly be interested in them. Where the Bible provides information about the authorship, audience, and historical setting of the prophetic writings, we should make use of this information in trying to determine their original meaning. Where the Bible is silent about such matters we should be cautious about any conclusions we draw. In either case we may legitimately reflect upon the meaning of the text for our own times.

According to a widespread judgment of modern biblical scholars, the prophets meant their words for a particular audience in a particular place and time, and we can understand the meaning of their words and judge their truth only in relation to their original historical setting. Their words are not directly relevant to other audiences. They have value for modern readers only as sources for understanding the history of ancient Israel. Any illumination we might derive from them for our own lives is accidental.

Many readers of the Bible hold an opposite view to this one. For them the biblical texts are a vehicle by which the word of God is communicated to faithful people in every age. It does not matter so much what the original writer intended or who the audience was. What matters is that these texts were preserved as the Holy Scriptures for the perennial guidance of the people of God. The process by which they were preserved and canonized is also not important. It is only important that they are in the canon of the Bible, that they are authoritative for faith, and that they yield inspiration and direction to those who read them with submissive hearts and open minds.

There are merits in both of these views. The first is correct in trying to determine the original meaning of the texts as the writers seem to have intended them. Many of the prophetic writings indicate that they were in fact meant for particular audiences. We will understand them better if we know who these audiences were and their historical circumstances. However, words can have meaning beyond the knowledge or intention of the author. Of course, if we take this approach, there is always a danger that we will read into them meanings that are purely subjective. On the other hand, it is very difficult to define objective limits to the possible meanings inherent in a text. Perhaps the best safeguard against subjective or arbitrary interpretation is not a set of criteria defined in advance but a continuing conversation among interpreters. If one can convince others of the plausibility of an interpretation, then it is not purely subjective.

*The Book of Isaiah* is the third longest (after the Psalms and Jeremiah) in the OT. It is more diverse in content and historical background than the other two so-called major prophets (Jeremiah and Ezekiel), and it is nearly equal in this regard to the Book of the Twelve Prophets. Its contents span a period of approximately two and one-half centuries (from ca. 740 B.C. to sometime after 500 B.C.). Many of the materials in chaps. 1–11, 13–23, and 28–32 appear to have derived from the prophet Isaiah, who was active in Jerusalem from ca. 740 B.C. until sometime after 701. According to an allusion in 8:16 to a binding-up of his testimony among his disciples, he himself was responsible for the beginning of the literary process that produced the complex collection we call the Book of Isaiah. Most of the remaining material in the book appears to derive from anonymous writers of the seventh and sixth centuries B.C., especially the sixth century. Chaps. 40–55 constitute a highly unified group of lyrical prophetic poems, written shortly before the fall of the Empire of Babylon to Cyrus the Great of Persia (539 B.C.). For lack of a better alternative, the writer of these poems is commonly referred to as the Second Isaiah. Chaps. 56–66 reflect conflicting religious perspectives from the early years of the second temple of Jerusalem (after 520 B.C.). Some of the poems in this section resemble those of the Second Isaiah (notably chaps. 60–62). Chaps. 40–55 are set against the background of the dispersion of the Jewish people, while chaps.

56–66 reflect the restoration of the cultic community of Jerusalem. These two groups of writings, together with the eighth century oracles of Isaiah, constitute the largest blocks of material in the book. Other, smaller blocks include chaps. 24–27, a group of eschatological poems from the fifth-third centuries B.C., and chaps. 36–39, an emended excerpt from 2 Kgs 18:13–20:19.

This vast collection of diverse writings has been arranged according to a threefold, topical scheme: (1) oracles of judgment concerning Jerusalem and Judah (chaps. 1–12); (2) oracles of judgment concerning foreign nations (chaps. 13–23); and (3) oracles of restoration and fulfillment (chaps. 24–66). This same scheme has been followed in the final edition of the books of Jeremiah and Ezekiel. It is impossible to determine whether all three books were arranged in this way at the same time, or whether one provided the model for the other two.

Almost nothing is known about the other contributors to the book. For all practical purposes, then, it comes to us as anonymous prophetic literature.

*The Book of the Twelve Prophets* is not unlike the Book of Isaiah in its diversity of literary types and its range of dates of origin. Most of the books of Amos and Hosea concern the northern Kingdom of Israel during its last quarter-century (ca. 750–725 B.C.). The oldest material in the Book of Micah deals with the southern Kingdom of Judah at about the same time, although many of the promises of hope in this book appear to be from a later time. Zephaniah, Nahum, and Habakkuk come from the end of the following (seventh) century. Joel, Obadiah, Jonah, Haggai, Zechariah, and Malachi are from the late sixth and fifth centuries, in part perhaps later. Little or nothing is known about any of these prophets, or about the circumstances of the writing or transmission of their works. The dominant theme of the collection is the pronouncement of God's judgment upon Israel and Judah. However, there are sections dealing with foreign nations (e.g., Amos 1–2, Obadiah, and Nahum). There are also many parts concerned with the future hope of the people of God (e.g., Hosea 14; Amos 9:11-15; Micah 4; Zechariah 9–14; and Malachi 3).

*The Book of Jeremiah* contains considerable information about the career of the prophet. He is unique in this respect among the OT prophets. Indeed, Jeremiah is the best known individual in the whole of the OT. The prose narratives and speeches in Jeremiah 26–45 contain a rich and detailed record of the prophet's life during the reigns of Jehoiakim and Zedekiah of Judah (ca. 609–586 B.C.). His call to prophesy is dated in the thirteenth year of King Josiah (1:1; ca. 626 B.C.). In about 605 B.C. he had recorded on a scroll the oracles he had composed up to that time (36:1-3). Many of the oracles now contained in chaps. 1–23 may have been on that scroll, though there is no certainty about this. None of the extant oracles can be placed with certainty in the time between Jeremiah's call (ca. 626 B.C.) and the time of the first dated material in the book (26:1; cf. 7:1; ca. 609 B.C.), however, it is possible that some of the oracles in the book may have come from this early period of the prophet's life.

In its canonical form the book has been arranged according to the threefold topical scheme which is also evident in the books of Isaiah and Ezekiel: (1) oracles of judgment concerning Judah and Jerusalem (1:1–25:13); (2) oracles of judgment against foreign nations (25:14-38 and chaps. 46–51; the Greek OT places these chapters together at the center of the book; this arrangement seems to antedate that of the Hebrew Bible); (3) prophecies of restoration for Israel and Judah (chaps. 26–45). Each of these sections contains materials of various dates, and they are not arranged in chronological order.

The editorial arrangement of materials in these three groups partly obscures one of the most distinctive literary features of the Book of Jeremiah. This is a combining of poetic oracles and prose narratives that is unique among the books of the prophets. The book is approximately half poetry and half prose. By contrast, the Book of Isaiah is almost entirely poetry, and the Book of Ezekiel, almost entirely prose. As a composer

of poetic oracles, especially oracles of divine judgment,
Jeremiah stands in the tradition of Amos, Hosea, Isaiah, and
Micah, the great prophets of the eight century B.C. However, he
seems to have been responsible, either directly or through
disciples, for the development of a prophetic prose style, which
is reflected not only in the biographical narratives and sermons
of the Book of Jeremiah, but also in portions of the books of
Deuteronomy and Kings.

It is uncertain exactly how much of the present Book of
Jeremiah derives from the prophet himself, or from his scribe
Baruch (36:4; and 45:1-5), but it is unlikely that any of it is more
than one generation removed from these two men. Thus,
whereas the books of Isaiah and The Twelve Prophets exhibit
prophetic traditions spanning 250 years, the tradition represented by the Book of Jeremiah spans only 50 years (from the
end of the seventh to the middle of the sixth century B.C.).
Despite the relative brevity of this span, the writers of the Book
of Jeremiah addressed two quite different historical situations
during that half-century. The first situation was essentially the
same as that in which Amos, Hosea, Micah, and Isaiah worked
a century earlier. These prophets spoke to a people who were
settled in their own land, governed by native rulers, and served
by long-established religious institutions. The activity of the
prophets was characterized above all by moral confrontation
with the leaders of Israel and Judah, who were wielders of
economic and political power, and could affect the course of the
nation's life and the social conditions of its people. The
Kingdom of Israel was destroyed by Assyria and absorbed into
its empire in 722 B.C. However, the Kingdom of Judah survived
until the beginning of the sixth century. During the first half of
his career Jeremiah prophesied to a society whose political and
religious institutions, geographical and economic circumstances, were fundamentally the same as those which prevailed
during the careers of the other preexilic prophets. Everything
changed half-way through Jeremiah's life. Jerusalem was
subjugated and then destroyed, and the leadership of the nation

was exiled. From 597 on Jeremiah addressed a disempowered and exiled people. Thus Jeremiah was a prophet of transition, with one foot in the monarchy and the other in the Exile. Ezekiel and Second Isaiah, who were the only great prophetic figures after Jeremiah, spoke entirely within an exilic situation (although Ezekiel, who was among those deported from Jerusalem in 597 B.C., did concern himself with the fate of Jerusalem and its temple until the time of their destruction).

*The Book of Ezekiel* shows us a different world from that of the preexilic prophets. As a result of his deportation to Babylon, Ezekiel was removed from the social setting that had called forth the oracles of earlier prophets. The people among whom Ezekiel found himself were powerless exiles. They were deprived of the institutions and responsibilities of a sovereign nation.

This changed situation is reflected in both the content and the form of Ezekiel's writings. The concise, poetic oracles which dominate the books of the preexilic prophets are gone, and in their place are expansive prose discourses, allegories, and visionary narratives. Much discursive prose is found also in the Book of Jeremiah, but the literary situation there is quite different from that in the Book of Ezekiel. In Jeremiah the prose stands alongside large collections of oracles in traditional poetic form, from which it is easily distinguishable, formally and substantively. Most of the poetry can be attributed to Jeremiah, while the prose must (I believe) be attributed to his disciples. The Book of Ezekiel, on the other hand, is almost all prose (the only major exception is a series of oracles concerning foreign nations in chaps. 27–32). There is no group of poetic oracles concerning Israel. Several scholarly efforts have been made to separate out a core of poetic sayings from the prose, but these efforts have failed to convince other scholars. The unity of thought and style in the book is too great. We are forced to view Ezekiel himself as a writer of prose, even though we cannot be sure exactly how much of the book comes from the prophet himself and how much from disciples or later redactors. The work of the latter consists largely of expansions of Ezekiel's narratives and discourses. Therefore, it is much more difficult to distinguish the various strata in the book than it is in the Book of Jeremiah.

The Book of Ezekiel is arranged in the threefold grouping with which we are already familiar: (1) words of judgment concerning the house of Israel (chaps. 1–24), (2) words of judgment concerning foreign nations (chaps. 25–32), and (3) words of promise concerning the house of Israel (chaps. 33–48). Chaps. 40–48 constitute a great blueprint for a restored, theocratic nation in Judah, centering on the temple of Jerusalem.

Many parts of the book are dated, using as a point of reference the first deportation of Judah. These dates range from soon after 597 (1:1) to about 571 B.C. (29:17). Thus, the book is thoroughly exilic in date.

The OT provides little explicit information about the literary process that produced it. Among the books of the prophets only one passage does this. It is Jeremiah 36. According to this account Jeremiah engaged Baruch, son of Neriah, to record on a scroll at his dictation the words of God that he had spoken "against Israel and Judah and all the nations" from the time of his call until that day, which was in the fourth year of King Jehoiakim (ca. 605 B.C.) He did this because he was debarred from prophesying in the temple of Jerusalem (36:5). Once the prophet's words were written down, Baruch read them in the temple (v 10). Eventually the scroll reached King Jehoiakim, who burned it column by column as it was read to him (vv 20-26). Therefore, Jeremiah dictated his oracles a second time to Baruch (vv 27-32). The text says nothing about the ultimate fate of this second scroll. However, modern scholars assume that it survived to become the nucleus around which the Book of Jeremiah grew.

It would be going too far to build a whole history of the prophetic literature upon this one narrative. Nevertheless, it seems reasonable to suppose that Jeremiah's experience was typical of the preexilic prophets. Isa 8:16-20 indicates that the prophet Isaiah also recorded his words as testimony for a later time, when he was frustrated in his efforts to communicate with the royal court of Judah and influence its actions (7:1–8:15). We know that Amos received a similar rebuff from the national leaders of Israel (7:10-17), although in this case the Bible does not say explicitly that he recorded his oracles as a result. Thus there is not much evidence to go on, but what there is is suggestive.

The prophetic movement in Israel emerged into the clear light of history in the time of Saul and David. Saul, who had some sort of encounter with a group of ecstatic prophets early in his career (1 Sam 10:5-13; 19:23-24), consulted prophets on the eve of his battle with the Philistines at Gilboa in an unsuccessful effort to divine the outcome of the battle (1 Sam 28:5-6). Then, according to the narrative, he resorted to a medium at Endor, who conjured up the spirit of the dead Samuel, by which he was warned of his impending defeat (vv 8-19). The picture of Samuel is somewhat confused in the OT. However, he was remembered in some circles in Israel as a forceful prophet. The rebuke of Saul contained in the passage we have just cited suggests as much. In the reign of David, which followed, we see the prophet Nathan exercising a similar function as a moral critic of the king (2 Sam 12:1-15). In this instance, when Nathan rebuked David for his adultery with Bathsheba and his murder of her husband Uriah, David accepted the prophetic judgment. However, later prophets did not fare so well as the critics of kings. The stories of Elijah and his contemporary Micaiah depict conflict with the royal house of Israel (1 Kgs 19:1-3; 22:1-28). Elisha was able to influence the course of affairs in the Kingdom of Israel, but only by participating in a bloody coup d'etat (2 Kgs 9:1-10). Our point here, however, is not to rehearse the entire history of relations between the prophets and kings of Israel, but merely to point to some of the narratives in the books of Samuel and Kings that illustrate the nature of the prophetic office during the preexilic period. The prophets seem to have been primarily the counselors and critics of kings and other leaders of Israelite society. Their word appears to have been delivered orally for specific occasions, either upon the request of a king or in response to a turn of affairs which in the prophet's judgment called for comment. The books of Samuel and Kings provide no information about the origin or development of a written prophetic literature. The only OT evidence of this process is contained in the book of the prophets themselves, and all of it except Jeremiah 36 and Isa 8:16-17 is inferential. Therefore any attempt to reconstruct the history of the literary process is conjectural.

The collections of writings of the preexilic prophets consist largely of brief poetic oracles suitable for oral delivery. With Jeremiah a new development takes place, namely, the creation of a discursive prose style, which constitutes approximately half of the book. Since Jeremiah did not himself write down his oracles (Jeremiah 36), we may suppose it was not he who was responsible for the creation of the new prose forms. It was probably Baruch or someone like him. We do not know precisely for whom the biographical narratives and sermonic discourses in the Book of Jeremiah were composed. However, the Book of Ezekiel, which is made up even more of lengthy prose discourses, mentions Ezekiel's communicating with Judean exiles in Babylonia, or with elders of the exiles (3:15; 8:1; 11:25; 14:1; 20:1). It does not say whether the materials collected into the book were composed for the use of the elders; however, it is not unreasonable to suppose that the forms exhibited here were developed in response to this new situation in which the prophet found himself. If this supposition is correct, it helps explain the shift in literary style, observable first in the Book of Jeremiah, from poetic oracles to prose sermonic discourses. The discursive, didactic style would have been more appropriate to the kind of intimate, sustained relationship between prophet and people referred to in the Book of Ezekiel.

The writings collected in Isaiah 40–66 are poetry. In this they are closer to the oracles of the preexilic prophets than to the prose narratives of Ezekiel and Jeremiah. However, these poems have been fashioned into larger literary compositions quite different from the oracles of the preexilic prophets. They seem to have been composed initially in written form for use with a new audience in the radically changed circumstances of the Exile. However, the information about this audience is indirect and ambiguous (e.g., it is unclear where the poems were written), whereas the Book of Ezekiel contains explicit notices about Ezekiel's location and audience.

For further discussion of the literary and historical aspects of the books of the prophets, readers are referred to the works cited in the Aids for the Interpreter.

# II. THE CALL AND RESPONSE
# OF THE PROPHET

Among the most interesting and theologically important passages in the prophetic books is a series of texts dealing with the call and commission of the prophets and the effect of these experiences in their lives. These are the only texts in the prophetic corpus that illuminate directly the prophets' understanding of their own relation to God. Thus they help us to see what it meant personally to be a prophet. Since there are prophetic dimensions in the ministry of the church in every age, a study of these texts may be helpful to those who wish to share this ministry. We may ask what bearing the role and experience of the biblical prophet may have upon the religious experience and ministerial calling of persons in the church today.

The experiences related in these passages contain elements specific to prophets, but they also contain elements that are universal, or potentially universal, in God's encounter with people. The Psalms are the principal writings in the OT that reflect the interior religious life. Some prophetic writings also do this, and the texts we will be considering here are the ones that do it most directly. These texts also contain a number of themes that occur in the oracles of the prophets, thus providing a kind of theological framework for the prophetic proclamation, and so they furnish a good starting point for our examination.

We will begin with the account of the call and commission of the prophet Isaiah in 6:1-13. This will lead us to consider, more briefly, the similar accounts in Amos 7:10-17, Jer 1:4-10, and Ezek 1:1–2:15.

The second part of the chapter will focus on Jer 20:7-18. This passage is one of the complaints (or laments) of Jeremiah. The others are 11:18–12:6; 15:10-21; 17:14-18; and 18:18-23. These five texts represent a continued dialogue between the prophet and God about the purpose of his vocation in the light of the persecution he suffered for his work. These texts are unique in the prophetic canon.

Next we will consider another kind of text relating to the role and activity of a prophet, namely, the prophetic sign, or symbolic action. These brief narrative passages raise further questions about the form of prophetic ministry and the relation of person to office in this calling. Finally, we will examine Isa 52:13–53:12, the famous poem on the suffering servant of Yahweh. This is the climactic word of the OT about the calling and experience of a prophet.

## The Call of Isaiah (Isaiah 6)

The best-known prophetic call-narrative has been a rich resource to commentators and preachers alike. It is vivid in its imagery, compelling in its dramatic development, and eloquent in its oracular climax. And it is so familiar and so powerful, it seems to preach—and interpret—itself. Therefore, it is a good text with which to begin. The reader will have enough familiarity with it to be able to follow readily, looking over my shoulder as I work with the text, and enough familiarity also to use critical judgment in assessing the interpretive moves that are made.

We need to do three things: first, determine what the passage actually says; second, reflect on its meaning in the Book of Isaiah; and third, interpret its meaning for us. In order to do the third adequately, we must do the first and second.

A fourth inquiry might also illuminate our interpretation, but it is not indispensable. This is to study what other interpreters have said about the text, either in the past or in recent times. If we did this thoroughly for Isaiah 6, the results would be voluminous. Some of them would be helpful while others would be historical curiosities. One possible benefit would be to discover whether the interpretation we regard as correct—perhaps take for granted, even to the disdain of contrary views—is a parochial one or is one that has received general assent. General, traditional assent does not guarantee the correctness of an interpretation, but parochialism surely calls an interpretation into question. Although it will not be our task to inquire into the history of interpretation, one should be ready to do this generally, with the aid of the commentaries, when this kind of help is needed in one's exegetical work.

Turning now to our first task, we ask what the text says. This assignment may seem too obvious to merit mention. Nevertheless, it must be done; and one should never assume that one knows what the text says until adequate homework has been done. I once heard a sermon on John 21:15-19 where Jesus asks Peter three times whether he loves him, and each time, after Peter assures him that he does, Jesus admonishes him to feed his sheep. The preacher asserted that the three words for love in Jesus' three questions were *eros, philia,* and *agape,* or sensual, fraternal, and divine love. This preacher had not done his homework! The passage does use *philia* and *agape* (in their verbal forms), but it uses them interchangeably. *Eros* is never mentioned, here or anywhere else in the NT. So the sermon misinterpreted the text. In this example the preacher would have had to consult a Greek NT, or a commentary on it, to determine whether the text could support his interpretation. He failed to do this; therefore his sermon was false. In some instances, it may not be necessary to determine what the original Greek, or Hebrew, says in order to proceed with one's interpretation. But, the least one can do is study several modern English versions of the Bible to be sure that one's interpretation is not based upon a dubious or eccentric reading. If all the reliable modern versions agree on the translation, one is relatively safe to proceed. If they disagree in substance (slight differences in phrasing or the choice of synonyms are unimportant), one should investigate further to find out why they disagree, and which of them is more likely to be correct (on which versions to use, see the Aids for the Interpreter). The first practical rule of biblical interpretation is, Never trust your favorite English Bible—uncritically!

Let us turn then to the text of Isaiah 6. In a rapid reading the nine major recent English versions seem very much alike. This is not surprising, for translators tend to be conservative about departing from the traditional wording of texts hallowed by usage, and ours is such a text. Nevertheless, closer scrutiny of the recent versions discloses some significant differences among them. I want to go through these in some detail as a case exercise. This is an integral part of exegesis and an indispensable basis for interpretation. I will not do a detailed review of all the recent versions for each text discussed in this book, but I want to do it once at the beginning to illustrate the process.

The nine versions constituting our translation-panel are, in chronological order, The Complete Bible, An American Translation (CBAT); the Revised Standard Version (RSV); the New American Standard Bible (NASB); The Jerusalem Bible (JB); The New English Bible (NEB); The New American Bible (NAB); Today's English Version (TEV); A New Translation of the Holy Scriptures According to the Masoretic Text, Second Section: The Prophets (NJV); and the New International Version (NIV). (An explanation of the grounds for including these versions in the panel, and excluding others, is given in the Aids for the Interpreter.)

In this exercise, and elsewhere, I will use the RSV as the base text; first, because it is the modern version most widely available to American readers; second, it is the English version with the best claim to ecumenical authorization; and third, it is unsurpassed among recent versions, all things considered.

In Isaiah 6, CBAT differs little from RSV. It places the last sentence of v 13 in brackets, thus suggesting that this is an editorial addition to the original text (NEB, NAB, and TEV do likewise). This is a question of critical interpretation, not of translation. You will not be able to resolve it merely by consulting the English versions, but will need help from the commentaries.

NASB also agrees almost entirely with RSV, though it has "temple" instead of "house" in v 4 and "repent" instead of "turn" in v 10. JB, TEV, and NIV also read "temple" in v 4, although the other five members of our panel read "house." Nothing major is at stake here, since we know from v 1 that the house meant in this passage is a temple (or sanctuary), as all nine versions indicate. Nevertheless, a check of the Hebrew text or the commentators would show that "house" is the literal translation of the original Hebrew word *(beth),* and "temple" is an interpretation. "Repent" in v 10 is not wrong (NJV also has it), but it does have a different nuance from "turn" which the other versions have. "Turn" is more general than "repent." Repenting is a particular sort of turning. The Hebrew word *(shub)* often connotes repentance; however, "turn" is a more literal translation. Thus, in both of the instances of minor variation in NASB it is evident that the translation involves interpretation.

The wording of JB is quite different from RSV. This should not surprise us, for, like the five versions in our panel which were published after it, JB makes no effort to preserve the literary tradition of the Authorized (King James) Version. Therefore we can expect each of these newer versions to have its own distinctive sound. Judging the sound and the other specific literary qualities of the versions is important in deciding which translation to read in public worship. However, it is not important in studying the meaning of the text. Most of the variations among recent translations are stylistic and not substantive.

In JB we encounter for the first time the use of the name *Yahweh*. The other translations use the euphemism "Lord" (in small capitals) to represent the original Hebrew name *yhwh*. Thus JB is the only version in our panel which follows the original Hebrew text literally (only the consonants of the name are contained in the extant Hebrew manuscripts, but it was probably vocalized "Yahweh"). Of course, this is not a translation of the Hebrew, but a transliteration. Deciding what practice to follow in this case is not a question of translation, nor is it really a matter of interpretation. Rather, it is a matter of liturgical tradition and religious sensibility, that is, habit and taste.

There are a few other significant variations in JB. It reads "be our messenger" in v 8, instead of "go for us"; "be converted" instead of "turn" in v 10; and "stripped" instead of "burned again" in v 13. The first of these variations is minor, since it is clear from the passage as a whole that the purpose of the going is to deliver a message. The second variation is perhaps not insignificant. At least the change to the passive voice contains a nuance that is not in the other versions. The third variation cited changes the image considerably. In the other versions it is of a stump that remains standing after a tree is felled and is to be burned out. This image is lost in JB.

JB does not have brackets around the last sentence of v 13, as several of the other recent versions do. However, it has a footnote explaining that this sentence is absent from the Greek (meaning the ancient Greek, or Septuagint) version of the OT. Here we have passed out of the realm of translation into that of textual criticism. Whether this sentence is indeed absent from the Greek OT is debatable (my own opinion is that the Greek OT presupposes the existence of this sentence in the Hebrew text from which the Greek translators were working), but the

..rpreter of the English Bible must turn to the critical commentaries for help in this case.

The sense of NAB is almost identical to that of RSV. The one difference that catches our attention is "purged" instead of "forgive" in v 7. Comparison with the rest of the panel yields the following result: CBAT, NASB, and TEV agree with RSV in translating "forgiven"; however, JB and NJV read "purged," while NEB has "wiped away," and NIV "atoned for." Thus all the most recent translations except TEV use a word with a ritual connotation. This is in keeping with the context. Therefore, even without a knowledge of Hebrew one could decide on the appropriateness of one of these alternative readings. (The Hebrew word means first of all "to cover over" or "make expiation," and to forgive is a secondary or derivative sense of the word.)

The next three versions, NEB, TEV, and NJV, present more serious problems to the interpreter than most of the ones we have been considering. NEB alters the sense of the passage at two points, vv 10 and 13. The other eight versions understand v 10 as an imperative. Thus the RSV:

> Make the heart of this people fat,
> and their ears heavy,
> and shut their eyes;
> lest they see with their eyes,
> and hear with their ears,
> and understand with their hearts,
> and turn and be healed.

According to this translation, the hardening of the people's hearts is the deliberate purpose of the prophet's commission. However, the situation is quite different according to NEB. It translates:

> This people's wits are dulled,
> their ears are deafened, and their eyes blinded,

> so that they cannot see with their eyes
> nor listen with their ears
> nor understand with their wits,
> so that they may turn and be healed.

This rendition changes the prophet's role in the transaction between God and the people. This translation should be more palatable to those readers of the Bible who regard the purpose of prophecy as bringing about repentance, and who are therefore offended by the idea that Isaiah might have understood his mission as exactly the opposite of this. However, all the other versions support the alternative translation, so one must be cautious in accepting that of NEB.

The second major difference in NEB comes in the final sentence of the chapter, v 13*b*. The whole verse reads:

> Even if a tenth part of its people remain there,
> they too will be exterminated
>   [like an oak or a terebinth,
>   a sacred pole thrown out from its place in a hill-shrine.]

In this rendition, the word of hope which stands at the end of the passage in the other translations disappears (RSV: "The holy seed is its stump").

I believe there is only one responsible course to follow here for the English reader who does not know Hebrew. It is to trust the majority of the modern translations, which is overwhelming in this case. Readers may assume that the NEB committee had *something* to go on to support their translation; however, unless the readers have the linguistic tools to assess the translation, they would be irresponsible to take the translation of NEB as the probable sense of the text, in the face of the overwhelming weight of contrary opinion on the part of the other modern versions.

TEV is a special case. In reading our passage through in this version we sense a greater degree of freedom. The entire wording is fresh and original. Rereading it, we see possibilities in the text which we had not seen before. However, a close comparison of the wording of TEV with that of the other versions has to evoke questions in our minds about the legitimacy of this version. Two examples should make the point. In v 5 TEV reads "There is no hope for me!" instead of "Woe is me!" At the end of v 13 it reads "(The stump represents a new beginning for God's people)." Neither of these is translation. Both are interpretation. Already, then, after studying just one major passage in the recent English versions, our suspicions should be aroused over the reliability of TEV for a close reading of the text. Its freshness and fluidity are attractive, and it certainly makes the passage easier to read than some other versions. But we have to wonder whether it makes it too easy.

Finally, in this last group, we come to NJV. Our attention is arrested in the very first line of the passage by the wording "my Lord" where all the other versions have "the Lord." This is appealing, because it makes the reference personal. Is it legitimate? One cannot be sure on the basis of the English text alone. It is clear that the Hebrew word in question is not *yhwh,* for if it were, "Lord" would be in small capitals, in this version as in the others. So it must be some other Hebrew term. This is as far as we can go without consulting the commentators and/or the Hebrew text. When we do this, we find that the Hebrew word is *'adonay* and that this term, very common in the Hebrew Bible, sometimes means "the Lord" and sometimes means "my Lord." Which is meant in a given instance is a matter of judgment, based primarily upon the context. Therefore, we may conclude that NJV's is a justifiable translation. I expect most readers will welcome this discovery. The second difference to command our attention in NJV occurs in v 3, where it reads "His presence fills all the earth!" instead of the usual "The whole earth is full of his glory." Once again we are forced to go to the commentaries to adjudicate this difference in translation. But even before we do this we can be led to reflect afresh on this familiar line. Is "presence" the deeper connotation of the term? Is "glory" merely the verbal and pictorial symbol of the indescribable presence of God?

In v 10 we encounter another substantial variant in NJV. It reads "Lest . . . it . . . repent and save itself," where the other versions read "Turn and be healed." This difference is substantial, exegetically and theologically. The text as it has been translated traditionally poses a serious theological problem to many readers. They find it difficult to believe that a prophet of God should wish to prevent people from being healed, and they are scandalized at the notion that this should be God's own sentiment. The scandal is eliminated if we follow NJV, for it is entirely conceivable that a prophet, or the God whom he represents, should wish to prevent people from trying to save themselves, on the ground that salvation comes only from God. What can the English reader make of this difference in translation? Our usual rule is to trust the majority when the vote is very one-sided. In the present case the vote of our panel is eight to one! Unfortunately, however, the vote is misleading this time. "Heal itself" is a literal rendering of the Hebrew text. This does not necessarily make the passive "be healed" wrong, but it certainly does support the legitimacy of the reflexive translation of NJV. However, there is no way that readers without Hebrew can know this, unless they happen to find a commentary that explains it. Otherwise they are helpless in the face of a difference in the versions that has significant implications for the theological interpretation of the text. One is led inevitably to the conclusion—and similar circumstances are repeated again and again in the OT—that every interpreter of the Bible should learn Hebrew! It is not necessary to become expert, but if one is not to be kept at the mercy of the English versions, one must learn enough Hebrew to be able to use a Hebrew-English lexicon and to check the text of the Hebrew Bible when one encounters major differences among the English translations.

The last variant for us to discuss in NJV occurs in v 13. By this time the reader may be confused by the variety of renderings of this difficult verse. NJV adds to the confusion. It reads, "but while a tenth part yet remains in it, it shall repent. It shall be ravaged like the terebinth and the oak, of which stumps are left even when they are felled: its stump shall be a holy seed." Much of this is familiar by now. However, the first sentence may be puzzling. Where did "it shall repent" come from, and what does the verse mean if this is the correct translation?

There is not much that English readers can do at this point, except perhaps wait for a new critical commentary that will explain this new translation in NJV. Most readers, therefore, will probably disregard this novel rendering and rely upon the old familiar one, which seems the most responsible course of action. The facts of the case, textually, are these: the Hebrew text has three verbs in immediate succession. The first means "to do again" or "to turn" (or "repent"), the second means "to be," and the third means "to burn." If one takes the three verbs together as parts of a single clause, then the traditional translation "it shall be burned again" or literally, "it shall again be for burning" is correct. However, if one takes the first verb as part of a sentence with the preceding words, and the second and third verbs as parts of a second sentence with the following words, then the translation adopted by NJV is correct. The textual issue is simply how to punctuate the verse. The Masoretic punctuation supports the former translation; however, this punctuation goes back only to the middle ages, and it is possible that the intention of the original writer was what NJV has taken it to be. The upshot is that, even if one is working with the Hebrew text, one is forced out of the realm of translation, where the problem is insoluble, and into the realm of interpretation. In this realm, NJV creates a serious exegetical problem. According to this translation, the prophet is commanded by God to dull the people's mind, lest it repent and save itself (v 10); but then, when he asks how long this shall go on, he is told that there will be widespread desolation and that when there is a tenth part left, it shall repent and then be ravaged (vv 11-13). Thus on the one hand, the prophet is supposed to prevent the people from repenting in order to save itself, but on the other, he is supposed to expect that a tenth (of the people, presumably) will in fact repent but be destroyed nevertheless. This is confusing. There are various ways one might try to explain away the difficulty, of course, but it is reasonable to ask whether we should even try to do so. The difficulty is created by the translation. If v 13 is translated in accordance with the Masoretic punctuation, that is, in the way all the other modern versions do, this particular problem does not arise at all. Thus the course to follow seems clear to me.

After struggling through the problems inherent in some of the recent English translations, the reader may have a sense of relief to discover that our last version, NIV, agrees almost entirely with RSV!

This completes our review of the major, recent English versions of Isaiah 6. It may have become tedious, and at some points it was certainly frustrating. I can almost hear readers asking, "Isn't there a simpler way to do this?" There is only one responsible answer, and it is no. Albert Einstein once said that he always made his difficult mathematical writings as simple as possible and no more! Greater simplification would mean misrepresentation. So it is with biblical interpretation. The textual problems are there whether we like it or not, and responsible interpreters have no choice but to acknowledge them and do the best they can.

When we have gone as far as we can in determining what our text says, we are ready to reflect about its meaning in the Book of Isaiah and its meaning for us.

The *meaning* of a passage in its original literary setting is not necessarily different from what it *says*. It is not as if the writer said one thing, but meant something else. On the contrary, we should begin by assuming that the writer meant what he said, and that his chosen words conveyed his intended meaning. However, in order to decide what meaning the text might have for us, it may be necessary to probe beyond or behind what is said into its implications.

Some biblical texts address us directly. Prov 15:1 is an example: "A soft tongue turns away wrath, but a harsh word stirs up anger." We do not need to know anything about the writer of these words (including his theology), or about their literary history, in order to determine their meaning for us. We need only to ask whether they are true. Have we found what they say to be true of our experience? Is this something we might find useful to remember?

Other biblical texts address us only indirectly, if at all. In these cases, we must ask about the presuppositions or implications of the words in order to know whether they have any meaning for us. So it is with Isaiah 6.

According to the text, the prophet saw a vision of God, enthroned like a king and surrounded by angelic beings. His first reaction was to sense his own uncleanness and that of his people. But next he felt himself to be forgiven and purged of his guilt; and then he accepted the invitation to be God's spokesman. Isaiah's commission was to harden the hearts of the people as part of the process of God's judgment upon them, until all of them had passed through the fire. When this was done there would be a possibility of new life in the land.

The vision is dated in the year that King Uzziah died, but we are not told here or elsewhere in the book whether the vision marked Isaiah's initial call to prophecy. Nevertheless, since the purport of his commission conforms to the heavy weight of divine judgment expressed in the surrounding oracles, we may conclude that it was a decisive moment in the formation of his self-understanding as a prophet and in his knowledge of God.

● Visions are intense human experiences which have happened to men and women in many lands and cultures throughout history, and they still occur today. Like all other human experiences, they are conditioned by the culture and society in which the subject lives. However, cultural conditioning does not invalidate the vision. There is no unmediated knowledge of God. Perception of the presence or providence of God does not always, or even usually, take clear visionary form in the mind of the one who senses this presence or this leading. Sometimes, however, it does, and whether or not the experience itself has the form of a vision, any description of the experience is likely to use images rooted in ordinary human life. Thus any verbal expression of an inward perception of the power or leading of the Divine, will be anthropomorphic, in one degree or another. Some expressions will be highly concrete and pictorial, like this vision of Isaiah's, and others will be more vague and ethereal. The authenticity of the experience as an encounter with the Divine cannot be determined simply on the basis of the accompanying images which are formed in the subject's mind. This can only be determined on the basis of the theological and ethical content of the subject's interpretation of the experience. The effect of a deeply moving religious experience upon the understanding, the attitudes, and the behavior of the subject provides the only possible measure of its authenticity as an *experience* of God. With respect to the authenticity of the *report* of a religious experience, that is, whether the experience reported actually took place in the consciousness of the reporter, cannot be determined by anyone else. We can do nothing but take the person's word that it happened.

We are curious to know more about Isaiah's vision. What was he doing when it took place? Was he awake or asleep? Was he in the temple? Had he had such an experience before? None of these questions can be answered. We cannot even know whether the prophet actually saw a vision as clear and vivid as the one described in the report. In short, we know nothing about the personal circumstances surrounding the experience and nothing about its psychological dimensions. We have only the report. As a result we cannot use the biblical record of Isaiah's vision to test the validity of the visionary experiences of other persons, past or present. Since we know nothing about Isaiah's visionary experience, but a great deal about the visionary experiences of other persons, we have to draw our conclusions about Isaiah's experience by comparing his report with those of other visions whose psychological concomitants are known. Thus the direction of movement in our interpretation is not only from the text to our own situation. It is first of all from the better-known experience of other visionaries to the lesser-known experience of Isaiah, and *then* to our own situation. Therefore, if we wish to ask whether it is possible for someone today to perceive the presence and leading of God in the way Isaiah did, we cannot answer the question merely by examining the biblical text and our own personal exerience. We know that the kind of experience Isaiah reported has occurred in the lives of other persons, both in the past and in the present day, because many others have reported such experiences of their own. According to the accounts in the OT, Ezekiel was more of a visionary than Isaiah. We will be studying two of his visions later, one (Ezekiel 1–3) in this chapter and the other (Ezekiel 8–11) in the next. We will have more to say about the nature of these prophetic visions then.

When we turn to the content of Isaiah's report of his vision, we find a compact religious drama, rich in its theological statements. The impression of God's transcendent holiness and sovereignty dominates the vision. Isaiah is overwhelmed by a sense of his own lostness and uncleanness and that of his people. Yet, while Isaiah experiences God as unapproachable, the seraphim declare that the glory (or presence, NJV) of the Holy One fills the whole earth.

This earth, which is filled with the glory of God, can become desolate because of sinful people (vv 11-13a). And yet, the desolation may be the prelude to a new beginning, "a holy seed" (v 13b). God endures through the desolation. The glory of God, which fills the earth, remains though nations fall, and is present for those who, like the seraphim, have eyes to see. Amid the passing of kings ("In the year that King Uzziah died, I saw the Lord," v 1) and kingdoms, God is still enthroned, in and beyond the world.

When the Holy God asks for a messenger to speak to the sinful people, Isaiah responds. As a necessary preparation for his mission, Isaiah's unclean lips are purified—by burning!—

and his sin is forgiven. The forgiveness is not merited by Isaiah. It is an unbidden gift.

His message is a hard one. He is to proclaim the people's moral blindness and hardness of heart; and the proclamation will only increase the blindness and hardness, until the people are beyond reformation and fall under the burning judgment of God. Will this burning be final destruction, or will it, like the burning of Isaiah's lips, be a purgation leading to a new beginning? The last word of the text suggests the latter. The painful gift given to the prophet will also be experienced by the remnant of the people.

What meaning can this text have for us? How, if at all, do we move from an ancient prophet's vision of God to our own situation? Are there aspects of Isaiah's vision that can aid our perception of reality or stimulate our awareness of the holy or guide our moral judgment?

• First of all, we must be clear about the elements of Isaiah's vision relative to his own time and place and which therefore may have nothing at all to do with our own. He spoke about the people of Judah in the eighth century B.C. as a people of unclean lips and heedless minds who were going to be devastated in their land and deported from it, partly as a consequence of their response to his prophesying. As it turned out, he was largely correct in his prophecy, although it took longer to come to pass than he seems to have expected. There may be parallels to Judah's national experience, but we cannot take Isaiah's vision as applying to any other nation than his own. It may alert us to look for parallels, however, and thus to examine more carefully the dynamics of social history.

Other historically conditioned elements of the narrative are the image of the heavenly court of God and that of a ritual purgation. These images are projections of monarchial rule and ritual practice as Isaiah knew them in Judah, and they do not reflect our own political and religious consciousness. If we are to identify at all with Isaiah, then we must demythologize the image of God as king and translate the act of expiation into more general terms.

What elements of the narrative can be generalized to illuminate our experience? There are several, though they must be taken as suggestive and not absolute, as invitations to reflect upon our own existence and not as self-evident principles of human life. And none of this will make much sense except to readers who share, or are disposed to share, faith in God as the primal source of all things and the ultimate arbiter of human destiny. With this attitude of faith, we may be able to put ourselves in Isaiah's place and relate his experience to our own. At least we can ask whether anything in his experience or understanding corresponds to ours or helps to clarify it or appeals to us as credible in the light of our understanding.

By reporting his vision as the basis of his commission, Isaiah affirmed the abiding presence and power of God amid and beyond the world. God ruled the course of history, called prophetic messengers, and forgave sin. One humbled oneself in awe and unworthiness before God, but responded in confidence to the assurance of God's forgiveness and in obedience to the urgency of God's command. This can make sense to persons of faith in any age, although a specific call to prophecy may be discerned only by a few.

The commission and prophecy in Isa 6:1-13 were meant for Judah in Isaiah's time. Yet its affirmation that new life may come to people as a result of desolation or, to put it in theological terms, that judgment can be a means of grace, is one that recurs often in the Bible and may be taken as a fundamental tenet of biblical faith. This affirmation has universal relevance.

The hope for Israel, according to Isaiah, lay on the far side of physical and social disaster. It involved stripping away all material supports, false gods, and political illusions. This was a hard road to renewal. We may ask whether the road to renewal for a community or a society always involves some sort of agony. Societies do not repent as individuals do, for the structures necessary to maintain them are so pervasive and complex that they resist change by deliberate effort. Real change often requires an inward crisis or outward calamity to provide sufficient impetus for it to occur.

Isaiah's call was apparently a unique moment in his life, a single inner experience so intense and vivid that it shaped the subsequent course of his life. He affirmed that God's glory, which is the symbol of God's presence, filled the whole earth, and yet he sensed the presence of God and its significance for him in a distinctive way in a single moment. Such experiences are not uncommon, although they are not universal, among the religious heirs of Israel.

Isaiah's willing, unhesitating response to God's call, "Here am I! Send me," is used frequently in the church as a model of obedience for faithful people, especially potential ministers. This use is not illegitimate, provided that it is qualified. Taken by itself and represented as the definitive model of religious or ministerial calling, it can be inhibiting to those whose sense of calling is uncertain or gradual in its development. The narrative of Isaiah's call should be set alongside those of other prophetic calls in order to give a fuller picture of such experiences. Jeremiah's call, e.g., was in marked contrast to Isaiah's. Jeremiah resisted his call and suffered persistent self-doubt in trying to follow it. We will study the report of his call below. Any use of such texts as models of behavior for persons today should be cautious and balanced.

In Isaiah's vision, God is king. The image is regal and masculine. Imagery of this sort permeates the Bible.

• The ways in which we imagine God are always conditioned by our culture. Isaiah's culture was patriarchal and monarchial. However, our culture is neither patriarchal nor monarchial, and we know that we must use other metaphors in thinking and speaking about God.

## The Call of Amos (Amos 7)

One biblical passage frequently throws light upon another. This is true whether we are studying individual words and phrases or larger units of the text. There are several other accounts of calls to prophesy in the books of the prophets, and it is edifying to examine them together with that of Isaiah's call. The earliest of these narratives is Amos 7:10-17. Amos was a contemporary of Isaiah. Although he lived in the vicinity of Tekoa, in Judah, he prophesied in the northern Kingdom of Israel during the prosperous and outwardly successful reign of King Jeroboam II. As far as we can tell from the internal evidence of his writings (which is all we have to go on), his public activity as a prophet was confined to the years of Jeroboam and did not extend into the time of troubles that marked the following decades. Isaiah's ministry, on the other hand, spanned both the time of tranquility and the time of troubles (the period ca. 735 to 700 B.C.).

As always, our first task in interpreting a text is to determine what it says. Therefore we should read it with care in the recent English versions. Readers may protest that this is a tedious way to read the Bible, and of course it is. However, we are not merely reading the Bible, but trying to interpret it. When one is reading the Bible for the main story line or for overall impressions, it is sufficient to read any one of the standard versions. Then as one moves to an ever more rigorous and detailed reading, where the homiletical, didactic, or theological use of the text depends upon a careful determination of its proper wording, one increases the intensity of study, including a more thorough consultation of the available versions. Thus one might adopt a three-stage strategy for reading the text. The first stage would be simply to read any of one's favorite versions. The second would be to read the two, three, or perhaps four versions which continued use has shown to be the most satisfactory. The third would be to consult the entire panel of recent versions, whether it be the nine I have selected or a larger group of the interpreter's own choosing.

At this time it is not necessary to go through the entire process of examining the nine versions of Amos 7:10-17. Instead, I will merely call attention to two lines in vv 12 and 14 whose translation affects our understanding of Amos' prophetic call.

First of all, let us set the stage. Amos has been prophesying in Bethel, the site of the royal sanctuary of the northern kingdom, that is, the Israelite rival to the primary Judean sanctuary in Jerusalem. The priest Amaziah considers Amos' prophesying to be destructive of public morale, and therefore a threat to the integrity of the kingdom. He warns the king about Amos and expels the prophet from the royal sanctuary, and ostensibly from the city and the kingdom. The charges he levels at the prophet and the prophet's reply have been the basis of a considerable modern discussion concerning the nature of the prophetic office. Therefore, we do well to consider these lines with care.

The issue in v 12 is whether Amaziah regarded Amos as a professional prophet, that is, as one who earned his living by prophesying. The issue in v 14 is whether Amos regarded himself as a prophet at all.

The most literal translation of v 12 is that of NASB: "Then Amaziah said to Amos, 'Go, you seer, flee away to the land of Judah, and there eat bread and there do your prophesying!" In other recent versions, the sense of the line is shifted. One shift is made by rendering the line, "Earn your bread (or living) there and prophesy there" (JV, NEB, NIV, and NJV). A further shift occurs when it is rendered, "Earn your bread (or living) by prophesying there" (CBAT, NAB). TEV goes even further: "Do your preaching there. Let *them* pay you for it."

Now, Amaziah's accusing Amos of being a professional prophet would not make it so. Nevertheless, if the accusation is there in the text, it is something with which interpreters must reckon; but if it is not, they need not do so. My own judgment is that the best translation here is a literal one. There is a genuine ambiguity in the original Hebrew line. Therefore, it is the responsibility of the translator to let the ambiguity stand. The freer modern translations remove this ambiguity. This is particularly true of TEV, which here as elsewhere is more paraphrase than translation.

What should interpreters do who do not know Hebrew? In

situations like this one should trust the more literal translations, namely, RSV and NASB. The translators of NASB in particular have made it their consistent purpose to hue as closely to the Hebrew wording as correct English will allow. As a result, NASB is the best English "pony" to the Hebrew text among recent versions (in this it follows its predecessor, the American Standard Version of 1901; another older version that is generally a good guide to the literal wording of the Hebrew text is *The Holy Scriptures According to the Masoretic Text,* of the Jewish Publication Society, 1917).

The issue in v 14 is whether Amos' reply is to be taken in the present or the past tense: "I am/was no prophet." Properly speaking, there are no tenses in Hebrew, so one must decide on the basis of the context whether the temporal reference intended is present or past. RSV, CBAT, NEB, NASB, and NJV understand it to be present in this case, while JV, NAB, and NIV regard it as past. If the tense is present, then Amos seems to be saying that he is not a prophet at all in the usual sense of the word, but merely a layman (a shepherd, as it happened) who was called by God to prophesy on this occasion. However, if the tense of the verb is past, then Amos appears to be saying that although he has become a prophet, he had not been one until God called him from his former work for this particular occasion. In either case, Amos is making two important points in response to Amaziah's effort to keep him from prophesying in Bethel. The first is that he is doing this prophesying because of a special commission from God and not because it is something he does habitually. The second point is that God has sent him to prophesy to the Israelite people, and on the basis of this authority he is prophesying in Bethel. The implication is that neither Amaziah nor his king, Jeroboam, has the right to prohibit him from prophesying.

The question of Amos' professionalism cannot be answered with certainty, in the face of the ambiguities in the wording of the Hebrew text. Nevertheless, regardless of the way one prefers to translate vv 12 and 14, Amos' account of his call depicts him as a layman, an amateur, who suddenly found himself prophesying in the principal temple-city of the Kingdom of Israel, because of a powerful sense of religious obligation. The narrative of his confrontation with Amaziah makes a further point. It indicates the kind of reception a prophet of God was likely to receive from the leaders of the religious and political community.

Isaiah realized in receiving his commission that his prophetic words would fall on deaf ears, and would even deepen the deafness. However, the Book of Isaiah does not say that he himself was suppressed or persecuted. In the case of Amos we see that his words were taken quite seriously, indeed that they were regarded as a threat to the security of the kingdom, and that as a result, his prophetic activity was suppressed.

Unlike Isaiah, Amos did not report a visionary call to prophecy. In the two narratives of prophetic calls which we are about to examine, we will see that one was visionary (Ezekiel's) and one was not (Jeremiah's).

The report of Amos' call is not as rich theologically as Isaiah 6. Nevertheless, several features of this narrative are suggestive as we ponder the meaning of prophetic ministry in the church today. Amos' message was one of moral criticism of the leaders of Israelite society and government, and a prophecy of dire consequences for their behavior at the hand of God. This message was viewed as a conspiracy, that is, as a threat to the status quo. In an age like ours, when people doubt the power of a prophetic word, this text in Amos serves to caution us not to underestimate the power of such a word.

There were ministers of God on both sides of the debate at Bethel. The priest Amaziah doubtless understood himself to be doing his work faithfully when he rejected Amos from the temple and the city. Of course, Amaziah was a member of the political and ecclesiastical establishment. Therefore, he was less objective and less free than Amos to discern a genuine word of God in the message of social criticism.

Regardless of the way we translate vv 12 and 14, it seems

evident that Amos was not a religious professional and had not been trained in prophesying. His call was spontaneous and his ministry was for a particular occasion. Ordained ministers in the church today occupy offices that are closer in function to that of the priest Amaziah than to that of the prophet Amos. This then raises the question whether it is possible or even desirable to combine the two functions into one. My own conviction is that both are indispensable to the vitality and authenticity of the church's ministry. It is less important who performs them that that they be performed. However, if the ordained clergy do not speak the prophetic word, it is unlikely in most congregations that it will be spoken.

## The Call of Jeremiah (Jeremiah 1)

Though biographical information about most of the OT prophets is scant or nonexistent, in Jeremiah's case the biographical information contained in the book is so copious, a volume the size of this one could be devoted to it. Therefore we are being highly selective when we confine ourselves to the account of Jeremiah's call in 1:4-19 and to one of his complaints (20:7-18).

When we take our usual first step in interpretation, which is to compare the standard translations of the passage, we find no serious problems with the text. There is almost complete agreement among the modern versions. The account of the call in Jer 1:4-10 is followed by two brief sign-narratives, describing experiences of Jeremiah that serve to confirm his sense of prophetic calling (the almond branch, 1:11-12, and the boiling pot, 1:13-19). One notable variation in translation appears in NEB in the statement of God's promise of support to the prophet as he discharges his commission. NEB reads, "I am with you and will keep you safe" (v 8). The rest of the versions translate, "I am with you to deliver you." The promise in NEB is more comfortable than the other, for being assured of deliverance does not preclude one's having to endure suffering and danger. The translation of the majority here turns out to be the better one in the light of Jeremiah's unfolding experience, and it is also a more literal rendering of the Hebrew word.

One other noteworthy English variant, this one supportable, appears in the sign-narrative accompanying the account of the call. The word play contained in the Hebrew of vv 11-12 is captured nicely by JB ("Watchful Tree") and NAB ("watching tree"). Some of the other versions explain the Hebrew pun in a footnote; however, these two manage to duplicate it in the translation.

Jeremiah's experience of being called to a prophetic career was apparently not visionary as Isaiah's. It is reported as a dialogue between the prophet and God. However, we cannot tell whether there actually were auditory elements in his experience or whether this is merely the form used to describe the emergence of his sense of divine vocation. Jeremiah did not step forward and volunteer readily for the commission as God's messenger as Isaiah did. Indeed, Jeremiah was a very reluctant prophet. We receive the impression that he felt compelled against his own will to follow this arduous and thankless career. This impression is confirmed by Jeremiah's complaints, as we shall see.

A major difference between Jeremiah's vocation and Amos' is that Jeremiah believed his whole life from birth to have been fashioned by God for service as a prophet, while Amos' report of his calling points to a brief interlude in an otherwise nonprophetic life.

We cannot be sure whether Jeremiah was a layman or a cultic functionary. Jer 1:1 places him among the priests of Anathoth, but it is not clear from this reference whether he himself was a priest or only his father Hilkiah. Since the office was hereditary, they may have both been priests. If so, this fact would distinguish Jeremiah from Amos, who was not a cultic functionary. Thus it appears that a prophetic calling could come to people in ancient Israel in widely differing circumstances and could occupy them in various ways for various lengths of time.

Apparently any faithful Israelite might be called to prophesy. If this was true in ancient Israel, is it also true in the church today?

According to the report of his call, Jeremiah's message was to contain words of both judgment and renewal (1:10). The element of hope is more explicit here than in Isaiah's call. Some interpreters have argued that this difference in the call-narratives reflects a difference in the message of the two prophets, namely, that Isaiah's was entirely a proclamation of national doom, while Jeremiah's combined prophecies of destruction and of reconstruction. A judgment on this issue is linked to the problem of the authorship of the oracles in the Book of Isaiah. In its canonical form, it intermixes oracles of doom with oracles of renewal, even within chaps. 1–11, which are generally regarded as the section most likely to contain the original oracles of the eighth-century prophet Isaiah. (Isa 2:2-4; 4:2-6; 9:2-7; 11:1-16 are all oracles of hope, while the rest of the materials in chaps. 1–11 are oracles of judgment.) Those who regard Isaiah's commission as entirely negative, and Isa 6:13*b* to be a secondary gloss, are also likely to regard the oracles of hope in chaps. 1–11 as not from Isaiah himself. On the other hand, critics are more inclined to attribute the words of hope in the Book of Jeremiah to the prophet himself and to see both doom and restoration belonging in the original account of Jeremiah's call. This view may be correct; however, it should be observed that the narrative of Jeremiah's call was as subject to modification by later editors as the narrative of Isaiah's call.

These considerations relate to the literary, or redactional, history of these two prophetic books. Now I want to consider an issue of another sort, which is involved in our interpretation of the calls of Isaiah and Jeremiah. This consideration is theological.

• Prophets are not only channels through whom the word of God is communicated to the people, but are themselves members of the people of God. They have similar needs and aspirations to those of other people. They are subject to the same temptations.

They are equally finite and sinful. Therefore, the judging and saving word of God is addressed as much to them as to others. Furthermore, the presence of God the prophets perceive, and the knowledge of God they attain, must be similar to the perception and knowledge available to every other human being. In the end there can be no radical discontinuity between the prophet's experience of God and that of other people to whom the word of God is addressed. If prophets know the presence of God as sustaining power and forgiving love, then this same knowledge is available to the people to whom they are called to minister.

The path to renewal may be quite different for a whole community from that for an individual, but it is questionable whether the purpose of God can be essentially different in the two cases. Therefore, any adequate exposition of the relationship of God and Israel would have to offer the possibility of forgiveness, reconciliation, and renewal. This does not mean that such a possibility must be explicit in every prophetic oracle. On the contrary, some prophetic oracles may be entirely accusatory and judgmental. Many such oracles appear in the Book of Isaiah and the other books of the prophets. However, oracles of judgment are rooted in a faith where hope is always implicit, if the experience of God is as it is described in Isaiah 6 and Jeremiah 1. A prophet could hardly perceive the presence of God as sustaining and redeeming for himself, and deny the availability of this resource to those whom he addressed. No message grounded properly in such experiences could be merely condemnatory. In the end it would have to be redemptive.

This means that whoever was responsible for the positive elements in the commissions of Isaiah and Jeremiah (Isa 6:13*b* and Jer 1:10*b*), and in the collections of oracles that bear their names, understood the prophetic experience and the prophetic word correctly. For the purposes of the church's proclamation, it does not matter greatly whether those who were responsible were the prophets themselves or others. However, I see no adequate reason, on the basis of a critical reading of the prophetic literary tradition, not to conclude that the initial responsibility lay with the prophets themselves. There are probably secondary elements among the words of hope in the books of Isaiah and Jeremiah, just as there are secondary elements among the words of judgment. However, this is not a sufficient ground for denying all the words of hope to the prophets themselves.

### Ezekiel's Inaugural Vision (Ezekiel 1)

In Ezekiel's call to prophecy the visionary elements are expanded to the extreme. The account of his call extends from Ezek 1:2 through 3:15. The vision is dated in the fifth year of the exile of King Jehoiachin of Judah (ca. 593 B.C.). A second vision, which occurred about a year later, is described in Ezek 8:1–11:25. These are supreme prophetic visions. The image in Ezekiel 1 of God enthroned and surrounded by winged creatures is clearly reminiscent of Isaiah's vision, indeed, we may wonder whether Ezekiel's vision was influenced by the Isaian tradition. However, it is probably sufficient to observe that both visions reflect the symbolism of the temple at Jerusalem, and it is probably the knowledge of that sanctuary and the habit of worshiping there that gave rise to the two visions, independently of one another. Ezekiel is identified as a priest (1:3), and this identification accords well with the priestly preoccupations that pervade the book, especially preoccupation with the temple.

Examination of the modern English version reveals no significant problems with the translation of this passage. Therefore, we may move at once to our reflections upon it. The narrative goes on at some length and in considerable detail to describe the winged creatures and the appearance of the glory of God, before any transaction takes place between God and the prophet. Ezekiel is overwhelmed by the stupendous sight and falls upon his face to the ground. Then he hears the voice of God addressing him. The spirit sets him upon his feet, and he receives his commission.

There is no experience of personal atonement in Ezekiel's

vision, corresponding to Isaiah's. He is simply lifted to his feet
and told to go and speak to the Israelites. He is told not to be
afraid of them, whether they heed him or not; but unlike
Jeremiah, he is not told that the basis of his assurance is in the
sustaining presence of God. He is not to fear the people, simply
because they are not fearful. He is told in effect, "Don't be
afraid of them. They are just a bunch of rebels!"

Not much is said about the content of his message. It is not
until a hand appears in the vision, holding a scroll, that any clue
is provided (2:10). The scroll contains "words of lamentation
and mourning and woe" (RSV). Ezekiel's reaction to this is
strange. Instead of the repulsion Isaiah felt to his commission
(Isa 6:11), Ezekiel eats the scroll (in the vision, of course), and
it tastes as sweet as honey to him (3:3). However, by the time
the vision has ended, the prophet is left bitter in spirit, and he
sits overwhelmed among his fellow exiles for seven days
(3:14-15).

There is no reference to the Spirit of God in the calls of
Isaiah, Amos, or Jeremiah. In Ezekiel's vision, however, the
spirit is a prominent figure. It is not identified explicitly as the
Spirit of God, although the implication is that it manifests the
power of God. Thus the relation of the Spirit to God is not
completely clear. The words addressed to the prophet come
unmistakably from God, but the spirit has a kind of
independence from God. Nevertheless, the function of the
spirit seems to be entirely to prepare Ezekiel for his prophetic
mission. Although the experience of his call is deeply ecstatic,
so deep in fact that he remains overwhelmed emotionally for
seven days, the significance of the experience does not lie in the
ecstasy itself but in the commission to the people that issues
from it. True religion, according to the biblical witness, is
always communal, even though it is deeply personal. Moments
in the religious life may be intensely emotional, even ecstatic,
but they are always to be appropriated for the good of the
people of God. They are not merely to be enjoyed in private.

Although Ezekiel's vision is as graphic as one can be, a

careful reading of the narrative shows that he understood the visual elements of the experience to be nothing more than pointers to the reality of God. God's being transcends human comprehension, and no image formed in the human mind can do more than hint at God's relation to human beings and the rest of creation. This is true of images formed in the waking mind and also of images seen in a dream or vision. This recognition of the incomprehensibility of God is implicit in Ezekiel's vision. Notice the care with which the manifestation of God's glory is described (1:26-28). The figure seated upon a throne is not that of a human being. It is nothing more than the likeness of the appearance of a human being (v 26). Thus what he sees is two steps removed from a human being. At the conclusion of the description the prophet wrote, "Such was the appearance of the likeness of the glory of the Lord" (RSV). The last word in the Hebrew text, of course, is "Yahweh." But it is not Yahweh whom the prophet sees. It is only the glory of Yahweh. And yet it is not the glory of Yahweh, nor is it even the likeness of the glory of Yahweh. It is nothing more than the appearance of the likeness of the glory of Yahweh! There is anthropomorphism here. However, the prophet has exercised great care in reporting the vision, so as not to violate his awareness of the transcendence of God.

It is interesting to observe how the prophet's ministry to the people of Israel is narrowly circumscribed. All he has to do is speak the word he is given. He is not to worry about how they respond. That is not his responsibility. He simply utters the word, nothing more, nothing less. There is no sense of pastoral identification with the people in this commission. The prophet's relationship to them is cool and distant, almost mechanical. There is no indication that he shares their situation morally or that he stands with them as one to whom the word of God is addressed. He is merely the transmitter of a message from God to the Israelite people.

In both Isaiah 6 and Ezekiel 1–3 it is acknowledged that the prophetic words will be delivered to a heedless audience. There is a difference, though, in the two acknowledgments. For Isaiah the blindness of the people was so complete that they were incapable of understanding his message and responding to it positively. They lacked genuine freedom of the will. For Ezekiel, however, the people's failure was more a stubborn willfulness than a psychological incapacity. They were capable of making the right choice, but they would probably not do so because they were so rebellious. In this respect Ezekiel was the most rationalistic of the OT prophets. He seems not to have acknowledged the bondage to which the human will is subject.

The call of Ezekiel contains many of the same theological and ethical implications as the other texts we have discussed, and these need not be reviewed. However, there are several other observations to be made here. Ezekiel was a priest who was called to prophesy. Since he was among the Judean exiles deported from Jerusalem in 598 B.C., he was separated from the legitimate Yahwistic sanctuary and was not able to function as a priest during the period reflected in the book. In other words, he did not combine priestly and prophetic functions into a single ministry. These occupied successive, rather than simultaneous, stages of his career. Nevertheless, by training and temperament Ezekiel was a priest. This did not prevent his becoming a prophet, even though his priestly theology and priestly sensibilities affected the way he perceived and proclaimed the word of God. One of the principal points to be drawn from a study of these and related prophetic texts is that the prophetic role is compatible with a wide variety of personal temperaments, professions, and circumstances. It is a ministry that belongs to the whole people of God, and at any given moment in that people's history the responsibility to fulfill it may fall upon anyone.

## Moses as the Prototype of the Prophets (Exodus 3)

Let us look briefly at a text in Exodus that is closely related to the prophetic call-narrative we have been discussing. Exodus 3 is the account of Moses' encounter with God via the burning bush at Horeb (or Sinai), the mountain of God.

It is impossible to date this text. It is part of the major narrative stratum of the Pentateuch frequently identified as the JE narrative (the narrative formed out of the combination of the J, or Yahwist, and E, or Elohist, traditions). Although the tradition that lies behind it may go back in part to the time of Moses himself, the present form of the narrative gives an idealized picture of Moses as a prophet of God. It seems to reflect a knowledge of the prophetic office as it was exercised in the eighth and seventh centuries B.C. by such people as Isaiah and Jeremiah. The picture of Moses' call and commission is a kind of synthesis of the prophetic calls described elsewhere in the OT. As is the case in the other call-narratives, the encounter with the Holy God is an intense experience emotionally. This is symbolized in the present account by the strange phenomenon of the burning bush. Moses expresses reverence before the awful presence of God by the removal of his shoes. We have seen that Isaiah cried, "Woe is me!" and Ezekiel fell stunned to the ground. Like Jeremiah, Moses here protests his inability to undertake the heavy commission that God gives him, but his protestation is turned aside by the assurance that God will be with him and will sustain him in the undertaking. Inspired by the encounter and emboldened by the promise of God's presence, Moses becomes God's messenger to the people of Israel.

The picture of Moses contained in the narrative of the Pentateuch combines a number of roles, or offices, ordinarily separate in Israel in historical times: prophet, priest, judge (i.e., legal arbiter), and chieftain (the precursor of the king in Israel). Thus Moses is made the prototype of the ideal Israelite leader. He is a kind of father to the family of God, or shepherd of God's flock. By providing this composite figure in the Pentateuch, the creators of the OT canon have legitimized these forms of leadership for the people of God, the covenantal community. This seems to imply that these are the normal functions of the pastoral office, whether they be exercised separately or in combination. The figure of Moses, then, serves as a kind of flexible, multifaceted model for the ministry of the people of God in any age. Exactly how and by whom these facets are to be embodied, whether by men or women, amateurs or professionals, ordained or lay, has to be determined in the context of changing needs and shifting circumstances.

## The Cost of Prophetic Ministry:
## Jeremiah's Complaints (Jeremiah 20)

Thus far we have been considering prophetic call-narratives. In their present form, they may have been influenced by the prophets' experience subsequent to the call; by and large, however, we must take them as reflections of the call-experience itself. Our next text is of a different sort. It is one of the so-called complaints of Jeremiah, and it deals with prophetic ministry in mid-course. It is interesting not only because of its place in the biblical tradition, but because the kind of experience it embodies can occur in the lives of the prophets in all ages.

There are five complaints of Jeremiah (sometimes dubbed his confessions). They are Jer 11:18–12:6; 15:10-21; 17:14-18; 18:18-23; and 20:7-18. We will concentrate upon the last of the five. Before turning to the text and interpretation of this passage we need to say something about the origin of these complaints and their place in the Book of Jeremiah.

These complaints are similar, in both form and content, to the individual complaint psalms of the Psalter. Scholars have raised the question whether there is any literary dependency between the two sets of complaints, and various answers have been given. Earlier in this century, when biblical critics were inclined to regard the Psalms as one of the latest segments of the OT, there were some who supposed that Jeremiah was the original creator of this type of material and that the complaints in the Psalms were influenced by his example. In more recent

times the dominant scholarly judgment is that the main forms of
the Psalms were created in the early monarchial period, if not
earlier. If this judgment is correct, then it is more likely that
Jeremiah's complaints were influenced by the Psalter forms
than vice versa. A few scholars have suggested that in content as
well as form Jeremiah's complaints derived from the older
complaint psalms. It has even been suggested that Jeremiah was
a priest who composed these poems for use in the rituals of the
temple, and that they are not personal reflections of his own life
as a prophet. This last theory, however, has been rejected by
the majority of scholars, who believe the complaints reflect the
prophet's own struggles, even though the literary forms and
some of the language has been influenced by psalms familiar to
Jeremiah in the temple. Whatever the origin of these
complaints, they are presented as the personal commentary of
the prophet upon the interior course of his life.

Like most of the other Israelite prophets, Jeremiah's words
went largely unheeded by his contemporaries, and he was
persecuted for threatening the Judean kingdom with destruction at the hand of God. The earliest dated account of the ill
treatment is contained in Jeremiah 26, which recounts an
incident when Jeremiah was preaching in the temple. A longer
version of the sermon is given in chap. 7. His address was taken
as a direct attack upon the temple establishment by the
prophets and priests who were the professional staff of the
temple. On this occasion Jeremiah's life was protected by some
of the lay leaders of the Jerusalemite community, princes of
Judah (26:10-19). This incident is dated at the beginning of the
reign of King Jehoiakim (ca. 609 B.C.). Later, when Jeremiah's
oracles of judgment threatened, not only the temple and the
religious establishment, but also the city of Jerusalem and the
Kingdom of Judah itself, the princes abandoned their former
virtue, and Jeremiah's safety was in constant jeopardy at their
hands (37:11-15; 38:1-28). These narratives provide a general
background to the complaints, which among other things decry
a plot against his life (11:18-23). However, we are not able to

place the complaints chronologically, either within the stages of Jeremiah's career as a prophet or among the known events of the history of Judah in his time. It would help us to interpret these laments (not to be confused with the Book of Lamentations) if we could date them more precisely. Do they reflect Jeremiah's struggle with his calling at an early time in his career, when he was not yet sure of himself and was less able to endure the persecution? Do they perhaps reflect doubt and anxiety that recurred over a longer period of time, even throughout his life? Unfortunately, these questions cannot be answered on the basis of the information in the Book of Jeremiah.

The uncertainty concerning which time in Jeremiah's life is reflected in these complaints arises in part from lack of information about his activities prior to the reign of Jehoiakim (609–598 B.C.). Although the prophet's call is dated in the thirteenth year of the reign of King Josiah (ca. 626 B.C.; 1:2, 36:2), none of the oracles is dated during his reign. Therefore, we cannot be sure how extensive a public career the prophet may have had during the remainder of Josiah's reign. The earliest dated prophetic materials are placed at the beginning of the reign of Jehoiakim, i.e., 609 B.C. (26:1). There are numerous references to the reigns of Jehoiakim, Jehoiachin, and Zedekiah (609–586 B.C.). We know that the public ridicule and persecution of Jeremiah extended throughout this period. However, since we do not know whether his public ministry actually began with the reign of Jehoiakim or much earlier in the reign of Josiah, we have a very uncertain background upon which to project Jeremiah's complaints.

The main point of interest to us would be in knowing whether Jeremiah eventually attained a sense of inner security and confidence in God, after an initial period of doubt and inward suffering brought about by his public rejection, or whether the doubt and anguish he experienced persisted throughout his life. Either outcome would be intelligible to us, and either would be useful in illuminating similar experiences in the lives of later

servants of the word of God. However, we simply do not know
which conclusion is the right one.

A plausible setting for the complaint contained in 20:7-18 has
been provided by the editorial placement of this passage
immediately after 20:1-6. According to this latter narrative,
Jeremiah was beaten and put in stocks on the order of Pashhur,
chief officer in the temple of Jerusalem, for prophesying the
destruction of the city. This event probably took place prior to
605 B.C., for Jeremiah was forbidden to appear in the temple
after that time (36:5, 9), and the prophecy that led to Pashhur's
order was delivered in the temple (19:14). The complaint that
follows is the last of the complaints of Jeremiah, in their
canonical order. However, we do not know whether this
corresponds to their chronological order; therefore, the
juxtaposition of 19:1–20:6 and 20:7-18 does not provide a
sufficient clue for dating of the complaints. Though the incident
narrated provides a plausible occasion for the complaint
immediately following, we cannot be certain that the two were
linked so closely in Jeremiah's experience. Since we do not
know the order of composition of the complaints, it is
impossible to trace any psychological or theological development in them.

These observations do not empty the complaints of meaning,
they merely set the limits within which we must interpret that
meaning. I believe the complaints express Jeremiah's struggle
to understand his calling as a prophet of God and to understand
and accept the suffering he experienced as a result of obedience
to this call. To say more than this, however, is to speculate in
the absence of any real evidence.

Let us look now more closely at the fifth complaint (20:7-18).
Four themes stand out. First, the prophet asserts that Yahweh
has seduced him, and he has allowed himself to be seduced (v
7). Second, he says that proclaiming Yahweh's word is the
cause of ridicule and persecution when he speaks, and inner
turmoil when he keeps silent. Third, the prophet pleads with
God for the punishment of his opponents, and he expresses

certainty over their eventual downfall, on the basis of confidence in God's justice. Fourth, he curses his own life.

The seduction to which Jeremiah refers is apparently his very calling as a prophet. According to the report of his call (1:4-9) Jeremiah understood it to be under the support and protection of God. Therefore, the persecution he experienced in fulfilling his prophetic vocation appeared to him to be a breach of God's promise. The suffering involved both humiliation in the face of ridicule and physical pain and anxiety at the threat of death.

There are several references in other complaints to the faithful service the prophet had rendered in obedience to his call (15:10-11, 16-18; 17:16-17; 18:20) and to the persecution he had suffered as a result of this obedience (11:18-19; 12:6; 17:15). These themes are not echoed in the individual complaints of the Psalter. There are frequent lamentations there over the sufferings of the righteous, and particularly the sufferings endured for God's sake. Appeals to God to effect justice are a prominent feature of the individual complaint psalms, and the plea to punish the workers of iniquity occurs frequently. However, the specific complaint over suffering for speaking the word of God does not occur among these psalms. Furthermore, the charge that God had deceived the prophet is distinctive of Jeremiah's complaint.

The fourth major theme of Jeremiah's complaint is the curse of his own life, a theme unique in the prophetic literature. Its only parallel in the entire OT is in the third chapter of Job, which many scholars regard as dependent upon Jeremiah 20. Since there are no parallels to this curse in the Psalter, we have no literary models to help us decide whether Jeremiah's curse is an integral part of the preceding complaint or an independent literary unit. The woe expressed in the second complaint (15:10: "Woe is me, my mother, that you bore me . . .") is related to the curse in chap. 20, although the latter extends the motif to the limit, cursing the prophet's very life. Thus we see that here Jeremiah gathers up themes found in the other four complaints; however, the intemperate accusation of God that

begins the fifth complaint and the despairing condemnation of
his life that concludes it, distinguish this complaint from the
others. Here the prophet's anguish reaches its depth.

There are several features of the other four complaints that
do not appear in this one. One is specific reference to the
identity of his opponents (11:21-23 and 12:6). Another is the
expression of general theological perplexity over the prosperity
of the wicked (12:1-2). Still another is the plea for God's healing
(17:14). Finally, there is God's reply to the prophet's complaint
(12:5 and 15:19-21). Thus the fifth complaint is not a mere
repetition of the other four. It shares several themes with them,
but it omits some they contain, and it includes some they lack.
This variety in form and substance among the complaints of
Jeremiah suggests that they do indeed reflect his personal
experience and his struggle of faith.

There are three variants in the modern English translations
of this passage that bear mentioning here. Several versions
translate the second verb in v 7 reflexively ("and I let myself be
seduced," CBAT, JB, NAB). This represents Jeremiah as
blaming both God and himself for his deception. The
implication is that although Jeremiah had sensed God's call as a
persistent leading from the time of his birth (1:4), finally he had
made the decision himself to accept the call. It was not a
predetermined destiny that he was powerless to resist, but a
vocation he was free to choose.

Three versions (JB, NEB, and NJV) translate v 9 in the past
tense, "I used to say, 'I will not think about him. . . .'" (JB).
This makes Jeremiah's anguish when not prophesying an
occurrence in the past rather than an ongoing experience.

The third variant to note here comes in the final line of the
complaint (v 18). RSV reads, "Why did I come forth from the
womb to see toil and sorrow, and spend my days in shame?"
Five other recent versions translate the last clause, "end my
days in shame" (JB, NEB, NAB, TEV, NIV; cf. NJV: "spend
all my days in shame"). This second alternative connotes an
irreversibility and finality that are missing in the other

translations. The Hebrew word readily supports the translation, "end my days." Indeed, it may even require it (the verb *kalah* means "to come to an end," "be finished," "be consumed").

What shall we make of this remarkable text? First of all, one is struck by the writer's fearless candor in expressing his pain and resentment toward God, a resentment mixed with deep perplexity over his calling and its cost in ostracism and persecution. The complaint is an excellent example of what today we call "being honest," i.e., giving free expression to one's feelings. If acknowledging one's feelings and trying to deal openly with them helps one to be a more mature and responsible person, with healthier, more constructive human relationships, then we can only applaud the candor of one who does this. However, dealing constructively with one's feelings, including those of anger, hatred, jealousy, and vengefulness, does not mean that one must give frequent reports to others on the state of one's emotions. Jeremiah confessed publicly to the extent that he recorded these complaints along with his oracles. However, judging from the picture of him in the biographical narratives, he was not known publicly as a complainer or an exhibitor of his personal feelings. His complaints are addressed to God; therefore, they must be seen first of all as episodes in his own inner life. They were made public only secondarily. We do not know in how wide a circle they were known, although my own guess is that it was initially only a small one including his friends and disciples, perhaps only Baruch, his emanuensis and biographer (see Jeremiah 36).

Jeremiah's complaints are not the only OT texts that exhibit candor in dialogue with God. The individual complaints in the Psalter are similar documents. As a model of piety these materials provide a correction to the habits of suppression and denial that often characterize the handling of doubt and anger by religious people. We tend to believe that such sentiments are incompatible with true faith and, therefore, we suppress them. However, they do not disappear, but persist in the subconscious

mind, often diminishing our self-regard and inhibiting constructive personal relations. The psalmists and Jeremiah
confessed their fears, doubts, and hostilities to God, even when
they believed God to be responsible for them! In my judgment
they provide an appropriate example for modern readers. The
alternative to fearless honesty is fearful dishonesty. Self-
deception can be destructive in the long run, whatever it may
accomplish at first.

Religious doubt frequently centers upon uncertainty concerning the existence of God or the reality of God's
involvement in one's life. However, these were not Jeremiah's
problems. For him God was only too real and too fully involved
in his life! The problem for Jeremiah was that he perceived God
as a kind of monster who deliberately misled him into a
vocation that brought nothing but humiliation, persecution,
and pain. His problem was not the fear that God was powerless
to affect the circumstances in his life, but the recognition that
God had the power to determine those circumstances, and did
so to Jeremiah's detriment. He could not understand why
fidelity in the service of God yielded no personal satisfaction or
blessing, but only sacrifice of all the comforts and joys of
ordinary human existence. Twice in his complaints Jeremiah
gave voice to what he believed God said in response to his
pleading. The first time it was an admonition to prepare for still
harder service (12:5), and the second time it was counsel to give
up self-pity and rededicate himself in service to the word
(15:19-21). This divine summons to a renewal of his obedience
was matched on another occasion by Jeremiah's own plea for
healing (17:14). These passages indicate Jeremiah's awareness
of his limited understanding and his need to put his destructive
feelings and doubts in a larger perspective.

Jeremiah's cursing his own life is not something we should
take lightly, on the ground that he did not really mean it. It
should be accepted just as it is, as an expression of genuine
despair. At the time when it was uttered the prophet saw life as
nothing but pain—no blessing, no joy, no fellowship with

others. The loss of fellowship is the extreme curse. In part this loss was inflicted upon Jeremiah by those who rejected him, but partly it was a self-sacrifice made freely in obedience to his calling (15:17-18). This word from a complaint is reinforced by the biographical narrative in 16:1-5. This passage relates Jeremiah's decision to forego marriage and the ordinary comforts of family, as well as other kinds of human association, because of the disjointed times in which he lived, and as a way of symbolizing that disjointedness in his own life. To Jeremiah it was an age of wrath, and he allowed the symptoms of wrath to show in his own person and life as a part of his prophetic witness.

Jeremiah's example of self-sacrifice, particularly the sacrifice of fellowship among the people of God, is an interesting one for the modern believer to ponder. One can understand a short-term sacrifice of this sort for the sake of a long-term goal. However, in Jeremiah's case the sacrifice lasted to the end of his life. Thus for him there was no final personal satisfaction to be gained by his sacrifice, nor did he have the consolation of belief in an afterlife. Such belief was not part of Yahwistic faith at that time. Thus Jeremiah was not motivated by confidence in eventual personal fulfillment for himself, but only by radical obedience to the word of God.

## The Servant of Yahweh (Isaiah 53)

Jeremiah's suffering as a man was a living-out of the story of Israel in his time. He himself experienced the deprivations of the age of wrath that was to come for the Kingdom of Judah. Thus the prophet's personal experience was a kind of incarnation of the judgment he proclaimed. This embodiment of the word of God in the life of the messenger is carried a step farther in the example of the servant of Yahweh in Isaiah 40–55. In the figure of the servant the conception of prophetic ministry in the OT reaches its highest development.

As an introduction to the discussion, I want to deal briefly with some sign-narratives in the books of the prophets. The prophetic actions described in these narratives are similar to the story of the servant of Yahweh in that the action of the prophet is a dramatic embodiment of the word that is proclaimed. In addition to publishing oracles, the OT prophets performed symbolic actions embodying aspects of their message. These symbolic actions took various forms, the most common reported in the OT being the momentary dramatization of a single word, usually a word of divine judgment. Ezekiel 4 and 5 describe a series of such dramatic actions performed by the prophet Ezekiel. They symbolized the impending destruction of Jerusalem. Jeremiah also performed several such signs (Jer 18:1-11; 19:1-13; 27:1-11; 51:59-64). The meaning of these symbolic actions was not self-evident. Each of them required some explanatory word from the prophet before they could convey the intended message. However, once understood, they provided a vivid, concrete reminder of the word the prophet wished to convey.

Some of the prophet's symbolic actions extended over a considerable period of time. Isaiah, e.g., is said to have gone half naked in public for three years as a warning of the future defeat of Egypt and Ethiopia (chap. 20). Hosea married a prostitute to symbolize the relationship between God and Israel (Hos 1:2). Jeremiah remained unmarried in order to symbolize the abnormality of the times (Jer 16:1-4).

Another lasting prophetic symbol was the naming of prophets' children. Isaiah named two of his children symbolically (Isa 7:3 and 7:1-4; Immanuel, in 7:14, may have been a third). Hosea gave such names to three of his children (Hos 1:4, 6, 9).

In most instances, it appears that the prophet actually performed the action reported in the narrative. However, in a few cases it is not clear whether this happened or not. An example is Jeremiah's burying of a linen loincloth in a riverbank (chap. 13). The long distance the prophet traversed in the dramatization, and the length of time between the two parts suggest that the incident was a parable told by the prophet rather than an action that he performed. Ezekiel's eating of the scroll in his vision (2:9–3:3) was the same sort of sign. It is not something that took place before the eyes of his audience, since it occurred only in his vision. It was only his telling about it that made it available to his audience. So it was with Jeremiah and the linen loincloth. Even if he actually journeyed the hundreds of miles from Jerusalem to the river Euphrates, as is indicated by the narrative, the journey could not be observed by his Judean audience. The point of the action could be evident to them only in the telling about it. Thus the narrative of the loincloth was really a parable and not a dramatized sign.

The unity of word and deed in these symbolic actions of the prophets is similar to the Christian church's understanding of the unity of word and deed in the life and ministry of Jesus. The OT does not represent the prophet as himself an incarnation of the word of God, in the way the church came to understand Jesus. However, the prophets' lives were bound up with the word in various ways. In some of the prophetic actions reported, the association between word and deed was brief and superficial. Here the prophet's behavior was nothing more than the public dramatization of an oracle. However, in other instances the link between the word and the life of the prophet was much more substantive. The principal example is Hosea's marriage. The most important relationship in Hosea's life became a lasting symbol of his message. His children, too, with their prophetic names, were incarnations of the prophetic word.

The symbolic action that comes closest to presenting the prophet as representative of the word he declares is Hosea's redemption and remarriage of his wife described in Hosea 3. Here the word of God's redemption of Israel is embodied in Hosea's redemption of his own wife. Thus he exemplifies in his treatment of Gomer the attitude and activity he believed God would make manifest in his relationship with Israel. The behavior of Hosea toward Gomer was only one episode in his life, albeit an important one. The whole of the prophet's life is not presented as an embodiment of the word of God. Thus when the church declared Jesus of Nazareth to be the word of God incarnate, it went well beyond anything suggested in the OT concerning the prophets. Nevertheless, some of the acts of the prophets are formative for the NT picture of Jesus as the Christ.

We turn now to the figure of the servant of Yahweh as he is presented in Isa 52:13–53:12.

The identity of the servant and the nature and scope of his mission are among the most controversial issues in OT interpretation. There is a vast scholarly literature dealing with these questions, and we cannot deal extensively with them here. Nor can we survey the numerous problems of translation presented by the Hebrew text, or assess all the variants among the modern English versions. Nevertheless, I want to include it in this discussion, for several reasons. The passage exercised a powerful influence upon the writers of the NT as they interpreted the meaning of the life and death of Jesus; and from their time until our own it has figured prominently in Christian theology and preaching. It is included in almost all Christian lectionaries, including the current Ecumenical Lectionary. Therefore, it is very likely to fall within the exegetical responsibility of preachers and teachers of the Bible.

● Since there are so many affinities between the servant of Yahweh in Isaiah 40–55 and Jesus of Nazareth in the NT, the Christian interpreter of this passage must take special pains to understand it within its own literary and historical context and avoid jumping at once to the NT parallel to find out what the text "really means." Texts can mean something to later readers that they did not mean to the writer or the initial readers, and it is quite legitimate for Christian readers to view this passage in Isaiah in the context of the NT witness. However, there is much to be learned by examining it first within the OT context.

I have already stated the major conclusions concerning the literary composition and historical setting of Isaiah 40–55. I regard the four so-called servant songs (42:1-4; 49:1-6; 50:4-9; 52:13–53:12) as integral parts of the book. One must take account of what is said about the servant outside these passages (e.g., 42:18-20; 44:1-2) as well as within them. The servant is Israel, God's light to the nations (49:6; 42:6). However, the historical Israel only partially fulfilled the mission God intended for it. This tension between commission and performance is reflected in the poems of Second Isaiah. Thus at times, and especially in the four servant songs, the picture of the servant is that of the ideal that Israel is meant to follow. At other times the writer refers to the actual Israel as the servant of God, and then the flawed character of Israel's service is acknowledged (e.g., 42:18-19). Or, the writer speaks of the servant as having a mission to Israel itself (49:6), because there are always many who fail to understand or perform the service that is meant for them. When the writer refers to the servant as an individual, he is personifying the mission of the people in an ideal, or representative, figure. This understanding of the servant makes the most sense, in my judgment, out of all that has been said about this figure.

The mission of the servant is prophetic. He is to bring justice to the nations and *torah* (divine law or instruction) to the remote parts of the world (42:1, 4). He is to enlighten the blind and free the captive (42:7). Thus the mission combines word and action, instruction and justice, enlightenment and liberation.

There are important similarities between the picture of the servant and the experience of Jeremiah. The servant was called before his birth (Isa 49:5), as Jeremiah believed he was (Jer 1:5). Like Jeremiah, he sometimes wondered whether he had toiled in vain, but he remained convinced fundamentally that his call and his reward were with Yahweh (42:4). Although he was persecuted, he found support and strength from God in his distress (50:7). Also, his mission, like Jeremiah's, was to affect nations and not merely Israel (42:6, cf. Jer 1:10). These are some of the more evident similarities between the two prophetic figures, and they make it clear that Second Isaiah's understanding of the prophetic office was in direct continuity with Jeremiah's.

Our designated text (Isa 52:13–53:12) is rich theologically. Its important implications for understanding the mission of the people of God command our attention and yet the passage is used so frequently in Christian preaching and teaching that it is too familiar. For this reason, it is difficult to avoid hackneyed comments or to say something that might catch the attention of an audience. Familiarity makes the greatest texts of the Bible difficult to teach or preach.

Close scrutiny of this prophetic poem reveals numerous difficulties in translation and interpretation, especially in matters of detail. Indeed, there are many more variants in this passage among recent English versions than in any of the others we have discussed—too many to be listed, let alone discussed. Furthermore, in many places, our usual reliance upon the majority of the modern translations leaves us uncertain about what the text really says. The footnotes and annotations in the English versions do not help much, nor do the commentaries. The divergence among the commentators on significant points is as great as that among the translators. What, then, is the practicing interpreter to do?

In a situation like this interpreters must take responsibility themselves for formulating a coherent interpretation, and for a text as long, complex, and important as our Isaiah passage this entails some hard work. However, the rewards are considerable, for one gains deeper insight into the meaning. One also gains a kind of independent authority in speaking about it that cannot be achieved in any other way. Thus our rationale for including this passage among the representative prophetic texts is partly to lead readers into an exegetical assignment where they must learn to be on their own.

What impresses me first of all in reading the passage is the sharp contrast between the meaning and value of the servant's life in the eyes of the world and its significance in the eyes of God. The servant has none of the beauty, wealth, or power people desire to make them happy and successful (52:14–53:3). Furthermore, the servant's life is filled with suffering and failure. He suffers the fate of criminals and outcasts (53:7-8), and those who see his misery and ignominy regard them as justly deserved punishments from God (53:4). However, God declares the servant to be righteous, his life to be the fulfillment of the divine purpose for him, and his ultimate vindication and reward to be assured (52:13; 53:11-12).

It is also remarkable that, although the servant is rejected, persecuted, and condemned, he is the source of ultimate blessing to the very people who treat him this way. Thus, the servant does not deserve the sufferings that come to him at the hands of the people, and the people do not deserve the salvation that comes to them through the mediation of the servant. Neither destiny is fair by ordinary standards of justice.

Another striking feature of the servant's life is his nonresistance to the treatment he receives. He uses no force to resist, but quietly accepts what happens to him.

The people declare that the sufferings borne by the servant were their own (53:4), as were the sins for which he was afflicted (53:5, 6). They assert further that his affliction brings them wholeness and healing (53:5). Correspondingly, God declares that his servant is responsible for making many righteous (v 11). In what sense are the servant's sufferings those of the people, and for which of their sins is he being punished? How does he bring about their justification? It would help us to answer these questions if we could first of all identify those who are speaking in vv 1-9 and the many to whom God refers in v 11.

It seems to me that the speakers of 53:1-9 are the many nations and kings referred to in the preceding verse (52:15). Vis-á-vis these many nations, the servant must be Israel, as he is identified elsewhere in the book (44:1; 45:4; 49:3). Therefore, the sufferings borne by the servant are those experienced by

Israel, and it is these that should have been borne by the nations. When we ask what specific sufferings Israel experienced in place of the nations, and what sins the nations committed for which Israel was afflicted, our text does not provide the answers. We must turn to the context of the passage in the book as a whole.

How the servant brings about the justification of many is also not explained in the text. The poet has God declare it to be so; however, he says nothing of how it comes about. We are forced to supply our own answer, hoping that our interpretation will not do violence to the text, even though it cannot claim its explicit support.

It seems to me that this passage makes the best sense if we understand the servant as one who declares the truth about God and the justification of the many as the appropriation of that truth. The clue to this interpretation is found in 53:11: "By his knowledge shall the righteous one, my servant, make many to be accounted righteous" (RSV). The servant's knowledge is knowledge of God, and the justification (or the being-accounted righteous) of the many is their attainment of this knowledge.

The text does not tell us what the servant does, what his vocation is, how he lives, or what his values, activities, and associations are. It also tells us nothing about his religious understanding, his theology, his faith. We must learn about these elsewhere in Isaiah 40–55, by studying all the passages dealing with the servant. He is described as God's messenger and witness (42:1-7; 49:5-6; 50:4). The message is everything about God and God's purpose of salvation expounded in Isaiah 40–55. It is not stated in Isaiah 53 that this is the case, nonetheless, I will try to show that it is implied in the overall development of thought.

Isaiah 40–55 is a theological unity. Whatever may have been the history of composition of the individual poems, they have been fashioned into a single proclamation, a remarkable witness of faith in God.

The principal theological motifs of the book are stated in chap. 40, which serves as an introduction to the work as a whole and which we will be examining later in detail. For our present purposes, only one point needs to be made: In the unfolding drama of salvation announced to Israel in its time of exile, an indispensable responsibility must be fulfilled by God's witnesses. Without them, there will be no understanding of the mighty acts of salvation that are transpiring in the people's experience. Indeed, since understanding is an essential ingredient of the acts themselves, the drama of salvation will not occur without it. Word and event are inseparable in the activities of God.

When Moses asked how he would know that God was present with him as he undertook to deliver the Israelites from bondage in Egypt, God replied, "But I will be with you; and this shall be the sign for you, that I have sent you: when you have brought forth the people out of Egypt, you shall serve God upon this mountain" (Exod 3:12). The saving presence of God is manifest in the historical event of deliverance and in the reflective act of worship. The act of worship bears witness to God and his word: faith in the God who has been revealed in the past (the God of the ancestors) and in the God of the future (whose promises provide goal and substance to the unfolding journey of the people). All this is signified in the revelation and recollection of the name of God, which is made to Moses as part of his prophetic commission (Exod 3:13-18).

Word and event, then, are inseparable. The saving event does not and cannot occur apart from the word that clarifies it as an act of God. The word, which calls for faith, precedes the saving event as promise and commission, and it follows the saving event as confession and act of praise. Without the prophetic witness of faith there can be no history of the people of God, since faith is the source and goal of the people's participation in the events that constitute their history. The people are not puppets manipulated unconsciously in a mock drama, but free persons whose acceptance of and participation in the providential destiny offered by God is necessary for that destiny to be unfolded. Faith in God precedes the saving event, thus the motive for leaving Egypt and going to the wilderness is precisely to worship God (Exod 3:18). Although Moses presents this motive to the pharaoh of Egypt as a momentary observance, an act that will require only a week's absence from Egypt, his actual intention is to leave with his fellow Israelites permanently. This is the true motive of the journey. It is to worship God.

Faith also follows the saving event, celebrates it, makes sense of it. Within the overarching purpose of God the escape of the Israelites from Egypt is completed when they worship upon the mountain from which Moses was sent to their deliverance. This act of worship also is an essential ingredient in the saving event, for without it the purpose of the journey would remain unfulfilled.

So it is with the new event of salvation that Second Isaiah proclaims. What this salvation will be is the subject of the entire series of poems that constitute the book. It includes releasing the Israelite exiles from oppression and breaking the tyrannical rule of Babylon. Furthermore, it involves proclamation of faith in the one God, Yahweh, creator of the heavens and the earth and redeemer of all people. It also involves repudiation of all forms of idolatry. It means beholding the glory of Yahweh in the drama of salvation (40:5), and it means joining in the universal celebration of God, which is the goal of the drama (chap. 55).

The prophetic witness is indispensable to the saving activity of God. Without it, the presence of God is not known within the life of the people, and the hand of God is not discerned in the course of their history. Therefore, already at the very beginning of Isaiah 40–55 there is a summons to the "herald of good tidings" to announce what God is doing (40:9). The servant of Yahweh is introduced to us at the end of the second major section of the book (41:1–42:4). Here faith in the God of Israel is contrasted with the idolatrous understanding of the nations, and the servant is exhibited as the one who, empowered by the Spirit of God, establishes justice and *torah* in the earth (42:1-4). Subsequent references to the servant make his prophetic vocation abundantly clear (43:10-13; 44:1-8; 49:1-6; 50:4-9). In some of these passages the servant is depicted as the individual model of the prophetic office, a kind of ideal figure, and in some of them the servant represents the actual people of Israel, who are called to bear witness to God.

The paradox of the prophetic vocation is that in proclaiming the knowledge of God the prophet comes to know God (43:10; 50:4). The knowledge of God is intellectual, of course, in that it involves understanding the ways of God and being able to communicate this understanding to others. However, it is more than intellectual. It involves the heart and the will as well as the mind. It is thus fully personal or experiential. It is a living, dynamic awareness of God and of oneself as a creature of God. The knowledge of God is attained partly by attending to the witness of others, i.e., to the prophetic tradition from Abraham and Moses to the present generation, but it is fully attained only by allowing it to become the ground and guide of one's whole existence. Thus word and life must finally be one. This unity is manifested in the story of Jeremiah, and it is also manifested in the story of the servant of Yahweh. In their lives, prophetic vocation and personal experience become indistinguishable.

The knowledge of God is the basis of health and wholeness; therefore, when the speakers in the fourth servant song affirm that the servant's afflictions have brought about their wholeness and health (53:5), it is not his afflictions alone that have done this, but rather the knowledge of God which is the basis of his entire life and for which he has been willing to suffer martyrdom. Merely being beaten and killed could not have brought about the well-being of those who knew him or observed him. It was the knowledge of God to which he bore witness and in which he lived that was the only possible basis of the people's health and wholeness. Righteousness, i.e., right living in relationship with God and other people, is grounded in and guided by the knowledge of God. Therefore, when God declares that his servant has made many to be accounted righteous through his knowledge, this can only be the knowledge of God.

Since the servant's prophetic vocation, which is identical with his life, is wholly dedicated to bearing witness to God and to the unfolding drama of salvation, the fulfillment of the servant's life and vocation is the acceptance by those to whom he is sent of his message and their appropriation of the faith that is grounded in it. Thus, when the people make the confession contained in this climactic servant song (53:1-9), the exaltation of the prophet that God promises (52:13; 53:11-12) is accomplished.

This interpretation of Isa 52:13–53:12 does not depend upon an exact determination of the original meaning of 53:8-9. It is debated by biblical scholars whether these verses describe the actual death of the servant or merely point to his being led up to the point of death. My own opinion is that the verses refer to his death, because of the clause "he was cut off out of the land of the living" (53:8), a phrase, which in Jer 11:19 must mean to be killed. Since other scholars consider the passage to be ambiguous, I would not wish to press the point of the servant's death. Whether he died or was merely brought up to the point of death, in faithfulness to his prophetic calling, is not important to the central message of the text. It may be important to Christian interpreters of the OT, who are concerned to draw the parallel between the experience of the servant and that of Jesus. However, I do not believe that a resolution of this issue is necessary to grasp the sense of the passage in its OT context.

• Second Isaiah depicted the prophetic vocation of Israel as he understood it in the sixth century B.C. In doing this he made reference to circumstances in Israel's life in that time, as well as to historic developments among contemporary world powers. These features of his writing are historically relative and do not bear directly upon the circumstances of the people of God or the

nations of the world in other times. However, the knowledge of
God which he proclaimed to Israel, and which he summoned
Israel to proclaim to others, is true in every age. We will be
dealing more fully with the content of this faith, as it is presented
in other portions of Isaiah 40–55, in subsequent chapters. Our
primary concern here has been to relate the life and mission of the
servant of Yahweh to the understanding of prophetic vocation
which is presented in the other books of the prophets.

I have asserted that the overall interpretation of the fourth
servant song presented here does not depend upon our knowing
with certainty whether the writer meant to depict the servant as
actually dying. Nevertheless, this is an interesting and
important question and is related to two others. The first is
whether the servant's triumph and vindication involve his
restoration to life, and if so, how this resurrection is to be
understood. The second question is What happened to bring
about the transformation of the people's perspective? What
brought them to an entirely different understanding of the
servant from the one they had originally?

The radical change in the people's perspective does not
appear to have been caused by God's ultimate vindication of
the servant, insofar as the latter might be regarded as a separate
event. This final vindication or triumph of the servant still lies in
the future, even though it is promised by God (52:13-15;
53:10-12). However, the transformation of the people's
perspective has already occurred. They confess right now their
new understanding of the meaning of the servant's life (53:1-9).
Therefore, this confession cannot be merely a response on their
part to an outward restoration of life, health, and blessedness,
that is, to an observable change in the outward conditions of the
servant's existence. According to the sequence of events
suggested by the text, the reversal of the servant's fortune
either follows the conversion of the people or is identical with it.
If the latter, then the servant's victory is an entirely spiritual or
moral one. However, the poet refers to the prospect of the

servant's long life (v 10) and prosperity (v 12). These should perhaps be understood literally and these outward blessings not taken merely as symbols—metaphors—of an inner, spiritual reality.

Whether the servant is depicted as being restored to life, or resurrected from the grave, depends upon whether he is described as dying. Perhaps we should think only of his coming very close to death, like the prophet Jeremiah (who was thrown into a cistern and left to die, Jer 38:1-13). On the other hand, it seems to me legitimate to infer from the language of 53:8-9 that the servant was actually killed. In either case, it is important to note that the restoration of the prophet is entirely God's work. The people have done their worst to destroy him. His deliverance from the power of death and his restoration to fullness of life come about solely by the will and power of God.

If the servant is a symbol of Israel—a kind of ideal representation of the life and witness of the people of God—and the story of the servant, a parable of Israel's story, then the servant's affliction and his restoration to life may be taken as symbolic of all sorts of concrete experiences in the historic life of Israel, and in the life of the manifold people of God.

The servant did not deserve the affliction he suffered, according to the people's confession, but they themselves did deserve to suffer in this way (53:4-5). Was his suffering vicarious, then, and if so, did it effect vicarious atonement? These have been important issues in the history of interpretation, especially among Christians, and they are valid issues for us to consider today. It seems to me that both vicarious suffering and vicarious atonement are depicted in this drama of the servant's life. However, I believe it unnecessary, and even undesirable, to interpret these terms in a mechanical or legalistic way, as has sometimes been done. What is suggested here is not the arbitrary or mechanical transfer of punishment from one person or group of persons to another, as if one's prison sentence were being served by another. Instead, we should try to understand these terms in the light of the experience of the prophets in Israel, and the experience of Israel among the nations. Not all vicarious suffering is vicariously atoning. It makes a difference how the sufferings come about and for what purpose they are endured. The servant was the prophet of God, messenger of God's word of judgment and redemption, teacher of God's *torah,* witness to the truth about God. The suffering he endured came about primarily because of his fidelity to his calling. According to ordinary standards of justice, obedience to God should be rewarded and not punished. Other people deserve suffering far more than the righteous servants of God. Indeed, others may deserve punishment doubly insofar as they are responsible for the sufferings of God's servants. These servants may be willing to suffer for their faith, partly for its own sake, and partly for the good that may come from their testimony and example. If this testimony and example bring others to an awareness of the truth about God, and thus to a truer relationship with God, then atonement—wholeness, fulfillment, righteousness, salvation—has occurred. Then the one who has made the witness to the truth, by word or example, can be said to have done so for the sake of, or on behalf of, the one whose understanding and life are affected. It is in this sense, it seems to me, that vicarious atonement is brought about by the servant of Yahweh. Regardless of whether the servant is an individual prophet like Jeremiah or a community of faithful Israelites in exile, the kind of communication and transaction symbolized in Isaiah 53 can occur.

# III. WORSHIP AND IDOLATRY

Worship may be defined in both a broad and a narrow sense. In the broad sense it comprehends the whole of religion, the service of God, and thus the whole life of the worshiper. In the narrow sense it refers to the performance of ritual acts. The second meaning is intended in the title of this chapter. However, worship in the ritual sense is inseparable from worship in the larger sense, therefore the following discussion will touch repeatedly upon the relationship of the two. Similarly, idolatry can be understood in both a narrow and a broad sense, that is, as false ritual or as false way of life.

According to Gen 4:26 people began to worship God in the third generation of humankind. Then, after the flood, the first thing Noah did was build an altar for Yahweh and present burnt offerings upon it (Gen 8:20). Abraham marked the journey undertaken in response to God's call by building several altars (Gen 12:7-8). Jacob is said to have established the first sanctuary in Bethel as a memorial of his nocturnal apprehension of the divine presence in that place (Gen 28:16-19). Moses told the king of Egypt that the reason for his request to take the Israelite slaves on a journey into the wilderness was so they could worship Yahweh their God (Exod 3:18; 5:1). When Moses and the Israelites later made good their escape from Egypt into the wilderness, they did worship God there (Exod 19; 24). A large portion of the Pentateuch consists of regulations for the proper performance of the worship, and this theme is a central one in the books of Samuel and Kings, and it entirely dominates the books of Chronicles. Many, if not most, of the hymns and prayers in the Psalms were composed for worship in the Israelite sanctuary, or were modeled upon compositions used there. It is clear, therefore, that public worship was one of the central realities in the life of ancient Israel. Indeed, without it Israel would never have existed as a people. Therefore it is not surprising that sanctuaries, sacrifices, priests, and ceremonials receive considerable attention in the writings of the prophets. In this chapter we will consider one major text from each of the four great books of the prophets. These texts are Isaiah 55, Jeremiah 7, Ezekiel 8–11, and Hos 5:15–6:6 (the last representing the Book of the Twelve Prophets). In addition several other texts will be treated briefly. Although united by a common theme, these texts differ greatly from one another in form, style, and imagery. They also come from a wide range of periods in the life of Israel, beginning with Hos 5:15–6:6 from the eighth century, and concluding with Isaiah 55 from the sixth century B.C. Thus our representative texts span the prophetic corpus, both literarily and historically, in relation to the theme of worship and idolatry.

## Jeremiah's Temple Speech (Jeremiah 7)

This chapter contains a brief sermon (vv 1-15) delivered by Jeremiah in the court of the temple at the beginning of the reign of King Jehoiakim. A narrative report of the event is contained in chap. 26. This sermon is the first dated public utterance of Jeremiah in the book. It is uncertain how much public activity Jeremiah engaged in before this time. Although chap. 1 dates his call seventeen years earlier during the reign of King Josiah, none of the extant materials are dated during this period, and there are insufficient internal clues among the undated oracles to supply the missing picture with any certainty. However, the prose narratives provide a fairly detailed chronicle of the prophet's life from the beginning of Jehoiakim's reign in 609 B.C. to the governorship of Gedaliah, sometime after 586 B.C. The famous scroll that Jeremiah dictated to Baruch is dated four years after the temple address (i.e., 605 B.C.; Jeremiah 36). The bulk of the oracles contained in the scroll may have been composed during this four-year period; however, it may have contained oracles dating from the reign of Josiah also.

It is uncertain whether Jeremiah prophesied publicly during the reign of Josiah; it is also quite uncertain how he evaluated the reform that Josiah carried out about 621 B.C. (2 Kings 22–23). This issue has been debated by biblical scholars, and no consensus has emerged. On the one hand, we may presume that Jeremiah approved the removal of idolatrous images and practices from the Israelite cult (2 Kgs 23:4-14), as well as the renewal of the covenant with Yahweh (23:1-3, 21-25). On the other hand, it is difficult to believe he would have approved the slaughter of the priests in the former Kingdom of Israel (23:20). It is certain, according to Jeremiah 7 and 26, that he rejected the superstitious regard for the temple that he found among the people of Judah at the end of Josiah's reign. This superstition must have been abetted by Josiah's reform, for the reform made this temple the only legitimate sanctuary in the kingdom.

An additional factor in the Judean regard for the temple and Jerusalem was the tradition concerning their deliverance from the Assyrian siege in 701 B.C. This tradition had grown to legendary proportions, until it was believed that Yahweh had delivered Jerusalem miraculously from the hand of the Assyrians because of the presence of the sanctuary there (Isa 36:1–37:38, esp. 37:36). Whatever may actually have happened to bring Sennacherib's siege to an end (2 Kgs 18:13-16 suggests that it occurred because of the capitulation of the Judean king Hezekiah), the people of Judah in Jeremiah's time were infected by the superstitious conviction that as long as the presence of Yahweh in the sanctuary of Jerusalem was acknowledged and the proper worship of Yahweh performed, the city, and the kingdom of which it was the capital, were secure. This is the attitude that Jeremiah addressed in his temple speech (7:1-15).

The issue raised by the temple speech was this: Under what conditions could the people of Judah continue to live in the land they had inherited from their ancestors, land long regarded as God's gift to Abraham and his descendants? Apparently many Judeans believed they would be secure in the land as long as the worship of Yahweh was maintained in the temple of Jerusalem. The temple address puts the matter differently. Mere maintenance of the sanctuary would provide them no security at all. Worshiping Yahweh at the sanctuary of Shiloh in an earlier time had not given the people of Israel any protection against the Philistines, as was only too apparent from its ruins that were still visible in Jeremiah's time (7:12-15). However, the people of Judah could expect to remain securely in their ancestral land, provided they maintained social justice and personal morality (vv 3-7). On the other hand, if they violated the moral and religious principles of Yahwism—as the prophet believed many of them were doing—they would lose possession of their land, and the temple in which they trusted would be destroyed (vv 8-15).

The professional temple personnel were scandalized by this speech (26:11), and they tried to put Jeremiah to death. Obviously, the prophet threatened their self-interest as officials of the religious establishment. However, the lay leaders of Judah, the princes (vv 16-19), saw no crime in what Jeremiah had done, and they prevented the priests and prophets from carrying out their wish. The royal officials of Judah appear in a favorable light in this narrative; however, we should remember, if we are tempted to compare the religious officials invidiously with the lay officials, that the latter proved to be equally selfish when their own interests were threatened by the prophet's prediction of the Babylonian destruction of the kingdom (37:11-16).

Before we probe the major theological issues in Jeremiah 7 we should do our familiar homework in the recent English versions. As it happens, we find only one significant variant among our panel of nine. In vv 3 and 7, where seven read "I will let you dwell/live in this place," JB and NAB translate "I will stay/remain with you in this place." A check of the commentaries will reveal that the consonantal Hebrew text will support either translation, that the vocalized Hebrew (Masoretic) text supports "let you dwell," and that the ancient versions of Aquila (Greek) and Jerome (Latin) support "dwell with you." The point is different in each case. In the first the prophet is asserting that the people will continue to live in the land of Judah if they obey the moral commandments of God. In the second he is saying that God will continue to be present in their midst if they obey the commandments. Of course, we cannot decide which translation is correct on the basis of our preference for one or the other of these propositions. Rather, we must decide which is more likely in the context of the rest of the passage. On this ground, it seems to me the preferred reading is "let you dwell in this place." The issue is not whether Yahweh will be present in the land, but whether the people of Judah will be there. Thus, when the prophet has Yahweh declare that he will drive the sinful Judeans out of his sight (v 15), as he has done previously to the inhabitants of Shiloh, the meaning is that they will be dispossessed from the land. Nevertheless, since there is an ambiguity in the text, it is probably best to consider both translations in relation to Jeremiah's prophetic argument.

The lesson usually extracted from this passage is that ritual without morality is unacceptable to God. As far as it goes, this seems to be a fair reading, provided that morality is understood both as individual uprightness and as social justice. This is a lesson taught over and over in the Bible, and it is not surprising to find it here. Nevertheless, this is not quite the same point

Jeremiah was making in his speech. He was not stressing the inseparability of morality and religion in true Yahwism. Rather he was saying that if the Kingdom of Judah relied upon the existence of the temple as the basis of its national security, while disregarding covenantal ethics, it could expect ruin. On the other hand, if the kingdom were faithful to covenantal ethics, it could expect to be preserved as a nation. This is the central issue to consider, and it poses two questions for us. First, was Jeremiah correct in his analysis of Judah's social and political situation? Second, does Jeremiah's analysis disclose a general truth about human communities that is applicable to our own time?

When we study the outward course of Judah's national history, it is evident she was a victim of the ambitions of the major powers of the ancient Near East. Located as she was in the narrow corridor between Africa and Asia, she was helpless throughout most of her history to resist control by the kings of Egypt and Mesopotamia. In the end, the only alternatives open to her were absorption into one of the great empires or vassalage. The great powers preferred to control the smaller kingdoms through vassalage, and resorted to annexation only when the vassals persisted in withholding tribute or disturbing the political and economic interests of the sovereign. King Ahaz of Judah led his kingdom into vassalage to Assyria ca. 735 B.C. (2 Kgs 16:7-18), and from that time on Judah was unable to determine her own destiny. She enjoyed a brief respite during the reign of Josiah. Assyria went into rapid decline as a world power after the death of Ashurbanapal (ca. 626 B.C.), and it was twenty years before another power was able to establish imperial control over Judah and the other petty kingdoms of western Asia. Babylonia achieved this hegemony in 605 when Nebuchadnezzar defeated Pharaoh Necho of Egypt at the battle of Carchemish on the Euphrates. During the interregnum Josiah mounted his reform, which was both religious and political. He managed briefly to reunite the central districts of the old United Kingdom of David and Solomon and to reestablish covenantal Yahwism as the sole legitimate religion. However, Josiah's dream of rejuvenating the Kingdom of David came to an end in 609 when he was killed by Pharaoh Necho at Megiddo. His son Jehoiakim enjoyed relative independence, as an ally of Egypt, until the battle of Carchemish. From that time on, Judah's destiny was determined by the neo-Babylonian monarch. At first Jehoiakim accepted vassalage, but in 598 he rebelled. The Babylonians subdued the rebellion, deported King Jehoiachin, who had succeeded Jehoiakim, together with most of the political leaders, the upper classes, and the skilled artesans to Babylonia. They set Zedekiah, the brother of Jehoiakim, on the throne of Judah as their vassal. A renewed Judean rebellion in 588 B.C. led to the final destruction of the city of Jerusalem and reduction of the Kingdom of Judah to provincial status within the empire of Babylon. This in brief was the course of national events during the life of Jeremiah.

Jeremiah's temple speech was delivered about 609, soon after the death of Josiah and the ascension of Jehoiakim. Reading Jeremiah's speech in the light of the international politics of the time, one may wonder what relevance Jeremiah's message had to Judah's national fortunes. Did the people's attitude toward the temple or their morality really affect their possession of the land or their political independence?

How shall we regard Jeremiah's contention that God would allow the people of Judah to continue in their ancestral land if they maintained their moral integrity and practiced social justice? First of all, we should acknowledge that Jeremiah viewed the course of national affairs, both Judah's and that of the other nations of the world, as under the direct control of God. Therefore, if Judah lost her political independence and her people were exiled from their land, these events occurred not so much because of the will of the Babylonian king, but because of the will of God. But if God willed this or that political fortune for the people, the decision would not be capricious. It would be a manifestation of righteous divine governance in their life, and this would be a response to their moral deserving. Thus, any major fortune in the life of Judah would be interpreted by Jeremiah and those who shared his prophetic faith as a blessing or punishment bestowed by God.

Was Jeremiah correct? The answer is both yes and no. It seems to me that the leaders of the Kingdom of Judah deserved the subjugation and exile that came to them at the hands of the Babylonians, though primarily because of their political folly. The state of morality and social justice within Judah had less to do with their political independence and continued possession of the land than their international politics. Nevertheless, these realms were not really separable. The political decisions made by the rulers of Judah were partly expressions of the moral and religious values they held and the quality of the social relations they shared. A leadership that indulged itself in a self-serving, magical view of religious ritual, and disregarded social justice and personal morality, was likely to make short-sighted, self-serving decisions in the realm of international politics. Thus, there is a sense in which the outward fortunes of the kingdom were the fruits of its religious consciousness and moral behavior.

• If we wish to apply the kind of ethical analysis Jeremiah made in ancient Judah to the circumstances of a modern nation, we must acknowledge the greater complexity of modern social and political life. What happens in national and world history today is the product of so many factors that it is almost impossible to comprehend what takes place, let alone control it. Simple moral explanations of the actions of nations and communities seem to have little place in our world. There are so many people, groups, and nations caught up in intricate networks of economic, political, scientific, technological, and cultural relationships; it is a wonder any sort of order and coherence is maintained in human affairs. Governments with the greatest concern for social justice may have the least power to effect it, and the well-being of nations may have more to do with the accidents of history and the possession of natural resources than with the religious life or morality of their citizens.

Nevertheless, prophetic statements like Jeremiah 7 continue to merit our interest and consideration. They tell us again and again to acknowledge the moral dimension in communal and national life, the importance of social justice for all members of the human community, the futility of all forms of magic and superstition, and the essential qualities of obedience to God. The religious convictions and moral behavior of a people have definite consequences for the life of their nation, even though it is impossible to trace them precisely. In this sense Jeremiah's analysis of the religious situation of his day has relevance in any age.

The subjects of worship and idolatry are treated not only in the temple speech, which constitutes the opening portion of chap. 7, but also in several other literary units that make up this chapter. Two of these (vv 16-20 and vv 29-34) contain comments on certain idolatrous religious practices current in Jeremiah's time, and a third (vv 21-28) refers to Israelite worship in patriarchal times. We will not discuss all these passages in detail here. However, the juxtaposition of these texts to the account of the temple speech suggests a question about the proper content of worship in Israel that deserves our consideration. In the third section (7:21-28) it is asserted that Yahweh had not commanded Israel's ancestors to offer sacrifices to him, but had required only that they follow in the way of life in which he guided them. This statement suggests that Jeremiah condemned the entire system of sacrifices, and thus called into question the whole content of temple ritual, which centered in the sacrifices. Furthermore, by placing Jeremiah's temple speech alongside passages concerned with the worship of alien gods (vv 16-21 and 29-34), the editors of the book seem to imply that the rituals of the temple were idolatrous. So we may ask whether the burden of these texts is the rejection of sacrifice, and the rites and ceremonies built around it.

We will leave the Book of Jeremiah for a time with the question of his view of the sacrificial system unanswered, and turn to another passage in the books of the prophets where this issue is raised quite explicitly.

## Mercy and Not Sacrifice (Hosea 6)

This text from Hosea contains the famous statement, "I desire mercy, not sacrifice; the knowledge of God rather than burnt offerings" (v 6). Many a modern reader of the Bible has taken this assertion, which we have quoted here in the traditional King James Version, as the true prophetic estimate of Israel's sacrificial system, or of any ritualistic religion. Along with Micah 6:7-8, this word of Hosea has been used to set the prophetic against the priestly tradition in the OT. It has also been used by Protestant Christians as a warrant for criticizing Roman Catholic sacramentalism. It certainly puts the question of the validity of sacrificial ritual very sharply and therefore provides a useful focus for our reflection about the shape and substance of worship.

The Book of Hosea provides no definite clue to the specific historical setting of this passage. When in the preceding oracle Hosea pronounces the judgment of God upon the kingdoms of Israel and Judah for engaging in warfare with one another, he seems to be alluding to the events surrounding the Syro-Ephraimitic invasion of Judah (ca. 735 B.C.; cf. 2 Kgs 16:5; Isa 7:1). This oracle ends with Yahweh's declaring that he will tear both kingdoms like a lion and return to his lair with the prey, until they confess their guilt and seek God instead of territorial aggrandizement. What follows next in chap. 6 is a confession by the people. Thus, the theme of confession provides a link between the two passages (5:15 and 6:1). It is not clear whether this is an editorial, catchword association or whether the two passages were meant by the prophet to form a unity. This ambiguity is reflected in the modern English versions. Some of them regard 6:1ff. as a continuation of 5:15 (CBAT, NAB, RSV), while others distinguish them as two separate passages (NASV, NEB, TEV, NJV, NIV, JB).

It seems likely that 6:1-6 is a separate oracle. In 5:15 Yahweh declares that he is going to wait for Israel and Judah to return to him, and the clear implication is that this means a return in genuine repentance and earnest confession. However, the confession of the people quoted in 6:1-3 is spurned by Yahweh as an ephemeral act of devotion (vv 4-6). Therefore, I do not see how we can take this confession as the kind of return referred to in 5:15. In any case, 6:1-6 can stand on its own as a prophetic commentary on the meaning of worship.

The people's confession expresses the heart of biblical faith: God is certainly present among them, and their fulfillment (healing, wholeness, vitality) comes about by living in the full acknowledgment of this presence. God had declared to Moses and to Jeremiah, among others, "I will be with you" (Exod 3:12; Jer 1:8). This presence was a reality not only for the prophet, but also for the whole people of God. The reality of God's presence that Moses perceived in the incident of the burning bush (Exodus 3) was the same as that perceived by the people at Mount Sinai (Exodus 19; 24). However, the moment of intense awareness of God differed from the rest of life only in its concentration. The experiences at the burning bush and the mountain pointed to the continuing presence of God, and the memory of them served as reminders of this presence. The awareness could be concentrated anew whenever the people assembled in corporate worship. The rituals of the sanctuary were the vehicles for recollection and celebration of the sustaining and saving presence of God. It was a distortion of Israel's faith to regard the sanctuary as the only place where one could enter into the presence of God, or to regard the traditional sacrificial rites as the necessary and sufficient means of appropriating the blessing of the God who was present. However, it was easy for people in Israel to slip into such misunderstandings, just as it is possible for people today to think of the worship of God as confined to sacred times, places, and rituals.

The people's confession, which Hosea records in 6:1-3, is in itself a fully appropriate expression of the relationship of God with his people, according to the prophetic faith. The prophet's objection to this confession, expressed in vv 4-6, is not over the intrinsic meaning of the statement, but over the people's inconstancy of devotion. Everything they said about God was true. Fullness of life was indeed to be found in his presence, and this presence was as available as any of the common phenomena of nature (v 3). But the God who provided fullness of life required steadfast devotion. This meant not only periodic public worship, but daily obedience to his righteous demands. Loyal devotion to God in all of life was so important that in comparison performance of sacrificial ritual was not important at all (v 6). This did not mean that sacrificial ritual was entirely unacceptable, but it did relegate it to relative unimportance as a means of communication and encounter between the people and God. It certainly made ritual an unacceptable *substitute* for steadfast devotion.

The term we have rendered "steadfast devotion" is the Hebrew word *hesed,* and it occurs twice here. In v 4 Yahweh declares that Israel's *hesed* is like a morning cloud or dew that disappears quickly, and in v 6 he makes the declaration "I desire *hesed* and not sacrifice, the knowledge of God rather than burnt offerings." In the modern versions the word is translated variously, "life," "mercy," "piety," "loyalty," "constant love," "goodness," or "steadfast love." It connotes both love, as strong affection, and steadfast loyalty; thus, it is lasting devotion. It is the kind of inward disposition and outward commitment that characterize family relationships at their best. It involves the heart, the mind, and the will, and it is expressed in deeds of love and service.

It is significant that the prophet placed *hesed* in poetic parallelism with the knowledge of God (v 6). The two are not synonymous, but they are closely related. We are reminded of the servant's knowledge in Isa 53:11, as the means by which many are brought into right relationship with God. This right relationship is characterized above all by *hesed.* The two terms

Hosea uses in this line express the two dimensions of faith: awareness of the reality of God and obedience.

Hosea's estimate of Israel's worship was largely negative. His words may fall short of utter rejection of sacrificial ritual as a valid means of corporate worship, but they certainly express grave doubt about it. Therefore, it is not surprising to find no mention of it in Hosea's prophecy of the future conditions of Israel's relation to God. He speaks of a ritual of words alone, without sacrifice (14:2).

This passage at the end of Hosea presents an important model for worship even though it is a brief one. The prophet is speaking about the age to come, after the destruction of the Kingdom of Israel. In the new age, when God would renew the covenant with his people and reestablish them in the land of promise (2:14-23; 11:10-12), their worship would involve confession of sin, petition for forgiveness, and disavowal of idolatry, both political and cultic (14:2-3). This is not a complete prescription for worship, but it is a significant beginning.

Hos 6:1-6 is not linked to the history of Israel in the same way as Jer 7:1-15. It contains a critique of worship that is applicable to all religious communities. It also expresses an understanding of the content and purpose of worship that can serve as a model in other ages.

### The Temple and the Glory of God (Ezekiel 8–11)

In Ezekiel 8–11, we return from Hosea's Kingdom of Israel in the eighth century B.C. to Jeremiah's Kingdom of Judah in the sixth century. Ezekiel and Jeremiah were contemporaries, though neither mentions the other. These chapters contain the second of Ezekiel's great visions (we have already examined the first in chaps. 1–3). The second vision presents a remarkable portrayal of idolatrous worship in the temple of Jerusalem, and it expresses the sensibility of a devout priest concerning the meaning of worship.

Ezekiel's vision of the temple took place ca. 592 B.C. (i.e., the sixth year of the exile of King Jehoiachin; 8:11), or about fifteen months after his first vision (1:2). He was in his home in Babylonia among the elders of the Jewish exiles when he experienced this vivid vision of idolatry in the sanctuary and of Yahweh's response in wrath.

As we would expect, Ezekiel's experience has been the subject of a considerable scholarly discussion, which has focused upon the question of how he obtained information about the rituals in Jerusalem. Some have argued that the vision was a genuine clairvoyant experience in which the prophet observed activities occurring five hundred miles away. Others have argued that Ezekiel made one or more trips back to Jerusalem after his initial deportation. Still others have concluded that he received reports of travelers from Jerusalem. A few have interpreted his journeying to Jerusalem as an experience of levitation.

My own view is that the experience was entirely visionary and that all the images were drawn from Ezekiel's own memory, supplemented perhaps by reports from travelers. We cannot determine to what extent his vision reflects actual rites and images used in the temple. King Josiah purged it of alien cult objects and practices in 621 (2 Kgs 23:4-7), and the accounts of the reigns of the subsequent kings of Judah in 2 Kings and 2 Chronicles say nothing about a reintroduction of idolatrous practices during the time the temple remained standing. On the basis of so little evidence, it seems best to regard Ezekiel's vision as a dreamlike amalgam of images and memories acquired in various times and places, including perhaps the pre-Josian temple, the post-Josian temple, and other sanctuaries frequented by Jews in Babylonia. Indeed, it is not necessary to take all the images contained in Ezekiel's vision as direct reflections of things he had seen in the Jerusalem temple. There may be purely imaginative features in this picture, in keeping with the character of dreams and visions. Someone who regarded the worship in the Jerusalem temple as idolatrous, as Jeremiah did, e.g. (Jeremiah 7), might have a dream or vision in which the temple appeared to be filled with images and rituals that actually had no place there. These would merely be the dreaming/visionary mind's way of depicting something that was not itself visible, or at least not visible in the same form. The dream/vision is not so much a photographic representation of the external world as observed or remembered, as it is a semiconscious dramatization of the dreamer/visionary's response to and interpretation of the world. One's *evaluation* of reality dominates one's dreams. The emotional element of dreams is usually high. The feelings expressed in them may be exaggerated projections of feelings experienced in waking life. Thus Ezekiel's vision may be regarded as an expression of his own interpretation of Judean worship and his intense emotional reaction to it.

The best way to account for the narrative in Ezekiel 8–11, it seems to me, is to consider it the report of an actual vision. However, as the account comes to us it presents a highly coherent and consistent drama, unfolding logically from beginning to end. Few dreams and visions are like this, and for this reason I believe we must conclude that the vision was reshaped when it was recorded. So what we have before us is a conscious, literary re-creation of what was seen in a vision. Some interpreters have regarded these chapters as entirely the product of literary imagination without any basis in visionary experience. However, there is no objective reason for denying that Ezekiel was a visionary, as the book reports; and it is entirely plausible to regard this narrative as a consciously polished version of a semiconscious, psychic experience. In any case, the principal responsibility of the interpreter is to perceive what is said, and implied, in the text; and to this task we now turn.

This bizarre, but remarkable, narrative unmistakably conveys the utter seriousness with which Ezekiel regarded the public worship of God. He treats it as a life or death matter. The horror with which he regarded idolatry is a measure of his awe before the majesty and holiness of God. True worship means life, idolatry means death, and the vision symbolizes this in two ways. First, the idolatry drives the glory of Yahweh away from the sanctuary, and second, the agents of death move into the city and slaughter the idolators. Significantly, they begin at the temple and work outward. The temple is the center of life, and the power of life and blessing moves out from the worship of God in the sanctuary to permeate all of the community's experience. Similarly, when worship is corrupted and falsified, it becomes the source of death—morally and spiritually—which works outward from the center to undermine and destroy the life of the community.

The picture of God's ordering the slaughter of every idolatrous man, woman, and child in Jerusalem is offensive to our eyes. Could God be so bloodthirsty? Where is the compassion and forgiveness other OT writers found in God? However, before we dismiss Ezekiel's picture as incompatible with faith in a loving, redeeming God, we should set the vision in its psychological and historical context.

Ezekiel's vision reflects the conviction that idolatry was destroying the Kingdom of Judah. He was outraged at this, and his anger was reflected in his vision. In the circumstances this was understandable. As a priest he had devoted his entire life to the public worship of God, and he had seen this worship used as an instrument of royal politics and self-interest. Judah was only a few steps away from national ruin, and for Ezekiel this destruction was the consequence of folly and idolatry within the kingdom. Judah and Jerusalem were about to die. Ezekiel had no doubt about this, and he interpreted this death as the outward manifestation of an inner corruption that had begun much earlier in Judah's life and progressed to fatal proportions.

● Modern readers may view the collapse of the nation as the final result of a long moral, social, and political process. However, the prophet Ezekiel viewed the destruction as an act of God, the divine punishment of a wicked and incorrigible nation. Ezekiel's picture of God's relation to the life of Judah is a highly anthropomorphic one. We may prefer to put the matter in nonanthropomorphic terms. However, if we believe God to be Lord of history, then we must find some way of accounting for the fall of Judah in relation to this divine sovereignty. We may be disinclined to interpret the destruction of Judah as simply and solely a punishment of God, as Jeremiah and Ezekiel did, but we may nevertheless be able to discern some moral coherence between the political policies and way of life of the Kingdom of Judah, on the one hand, and the kingdom's fate on the other.

Ezekiel's vision of the temple and the glory of God is a memorable essay on the presence and power of God. The fundamental promise of God to his people was "I will be with you" (Exod 3:12). How was this presence known? How should the people respond to it? What function did the sanctuary have in the recognition and appropriation of this presence? These are questions raised by Ezekiel's vision, and they are central to the understanding of every religious community.

People in the biblical world, and in other times and places, experienced certain places as holy, i.e., they sensed them as invested with extraordinary power. This power was potentially beneficial, but it could also be dangerous if it were treated inappropriately. Priesthoods, sanctuaries, liturgical calendars, laws of sacrifice, rules of access and proscription, prayers and incantations were all devised and maintained in order to manage the extraordinary power available in the holy place and to channel it into various forms of blessing.

Few of Israel's rituals and few of her holy places were distinctively Israelite, or Yahwistic. Much of her cultic life was indistinguishable from that of the surrounding peoples. Much of the ritual of the altar was the legacy of pre-Israelite times, and its original purpose or rationale had long been forgotten. Thus, they are unexplained in the biblical tradition. Most of this legacy seemed compatible with Yahwistic faith, in the minds of those who shaped the pentateuchal tradition. However, a few features of popular religious practice, such as the use of plastic images to represent the deity and the ritual dramas based upon polytheistic deification of the forces of nature, with their mythology of divine warfare, sexual procreation, and sensual seasonal rituals, were intolerable to Yahwistic faith. However, some of the seasonal festivals were demythologized and reinterpreted as responses to the blessings of God in history and nature. An elaborate system of animal sacrifices, common to most popular religion, was retained.

Ritual played a far greater part in the life of ancient people than it does in ours. Modern Western people regard nature as autonomous and self-regulating, and they regard history solely as a process of human interaction. There is no room in the modern view for superhuman or supernatural forces. To be sure, the forces and processes of nature transcend human power and understanding, but our means of dealing with the limitations of our power and knowledge is to develop new technology and promote science. Ritual means of controlling or placating powers greater than ourselves are obsolete.

International relations are another area in which ancient people resorted routinely to divine aid, but which for us are a matter of purely human (or secular) concern. In the next chapter we will discuss the oracles concerning foreign nations that comprise a substantial portion of the books of the prophets. We will see in these oracles how Israel's prophets understood the role of the divine in her international politics. To a considerable extent they desacralized and deritualized politics, just as they desacralized many other areas of human activity. In this respect our modern perspective on nature and history has been deeply influenced by prophetic teaching, and their critique of ritual, and the theology infusing it, was a potent factor. A major difference between the prophets' perspective and that of many modern people is that the prophets' critique of ritual and their desacralization of nature were called forth by their faith in God, whereas the modern perspective is often a mere secularism in which faith in God plays no part. In modern secular perspective the powers that make up people's environment and shape their destiny are entirely natural and human; in ancient perspective they were largely divine. Thus, the choice for ancient Israelites, as they tried to relate to powers greater than themselves, was not between God and no God, but between God and other gods. Every aspect of life was believed to be permeated by divine power or subject to the will of divine beings. Therefore, one had constantly to deal with these powers in some appropriate way, so ritualism was a way of life for everyone. Changes of the seasons, months, and days were marked by private and public rituals. No major enterprise was undertaken without first seeking divine blessing or attempting to ascertain the outcome in relation to the will of the gods. Every turn of fortune, both good and ill, required an appropriate ritual response. Responses to good fortune were meant to preserve it, while responses to ill fortune were meant to reverse it. Sanctuaries, priests, and seers were ubiquitous, for they were thought indispensable to survival.

When King Josiah centralized public worship in Israel, destroying every sanctuary except the temple in Jerusalem, and prohibiting even the legitimate priests of Yahweh from performing rituals anywhere but in this one national sanctuary, he went squarely against the grain of all ancient life and culture, including that of the people of Israel. The project was doomed to failure. Popular faith conflicted too much with the theology behind the reform, and the need for ritual in daily life was too great.

When Ezekiel envisioned the departure of the glory of Yahweh from the temple and city of Jerusalem (10:18-22; 11:22-25), he foresaw for the people of Jerusalem a religious situation that had already come to pass for other Israelite communities during Josiah's reign. This was the experience of being denied access to the ritual presence of Yahweh. In their minds the power of blessing had been removed from their midst and from their control. Ezekiel foresaw this process carried to its conclusion, where the entire people of Israel would be deprived of the tabernacaling glory of God.

In his vision Ezekiel saw the people of Jerusalem practicing a variety of idolatrous rites (8:5-17) and saw that these idolatries were the cause of God's punishment of the people. The punishment was two-fold: the slaughter of the idolators themselves and the removal of the glory of God from the temple. In reporting this vision to the elders of Israel, Ezekiel not only described his own moral and emotional response to the religious situation in Jerusalem, but he also provided a parable of the story of Israel and Yahweh.

Ezekiel's vision lends itself to several possible interpretations. One might analyze it, like any other vision or dream, as a reflection of Ezekiel's own feelings, experiences, and perceptions. It certainly manifests the horror a devout priest of Yahweh would feel toward popular religious idolatry in Judah, and the rage these practices would provoke in him. Though correct as far as it goes, such an analysis would not be sufficient, for Ezekiel's report of the vision was presented as a prophetic statement with regard to the inner corruption and outward destruction of the temple and the city of Jerusalem. It may originally have been a prophecy of their final destruction, but it was also an interpretation of the cause of that destruction. Beyond its personal meaning for Ezekiel and its historic meaning for the people of Judah, the vision ought to be provocative to congregations in the present. It serves as a kind of negative image against which to measure the religious situation within our communities, or at least to raise significant questions concerning the moral and religious condition of our own sanctuaries, whatever they may be. What idolatries in our own religious practice, or in the practice of our nation, capture us in the way the people of Judah were captured? What are the moral and social consequences? Is anyone immune from these consequences? Is anyone innocent of the idolatry? Are there any remedies? Can the redemptive power of God break through before it is too late? Are worship and idolatry matters of life and death in our time as they were in Ezekiel's? Was this visionary prophet a fanatic or a realist? How does the glory of God manifest itself? What is the relation of the glory to the presence and power of God? How should the people respond to the presence, and how may they rightly appropriate the power? Isaiah saw the glory of God as filling the whole earth (6:3), while Ezekiel located the glory primarily in the sanctuary. Perhaps we must perceive the glory of God in both realms before we can do so in either. Indeed, Isaiah's vision suggests this to be true, for the affirmation that God's glory fills the whole earth is made by those who stand in the presence of God in the sanctuary.

## Seeking God in Exile (Jeremiah 29)

For ancient Israel, seeking God meant primarily going to a sanctuary and engaging in a private or public ritual. Although the Holy might manifest itself anywhere at any time, this happened most frequently and predictably in conjunction with acts of worship performed at places and in ways hallowed by ancient usage and made familiar by long habit. The experience of the Holy is a sign of the presence of God, or at least of the conscious recognition of his presence. The Holy One whose presence is acknowledged in the act of worship is the source of blessing, but sensing the presence of the Holy One, i.e., the experience of encounter itself, is also a blessing. Indeed, it may be the supreme blessing. Thus for the writers of psalms 42 and 137, to be denied participation in worship in accustomed places and traditional ways was to be denied the primary source of happiness and peace. For a faithful Judean, exile from Jerusalem and the temple meant separation from the sanctifying presence of God. In Ezekiel's vision the glory of God left the temple and the city, but this did not signify that the glory—or the presence it symbolized—would be subsequently manifest in the places of Israel's exile. It would not be manifest at all, at least not in any way that would make blessing available to the people. According to the prophet, Yahweh's glory would return when the city of Jerusalem and its temple were restored and purified (43:1-7). This prophecy is part of the larger picture of the future establishment of a theocratic kingdom which occupies Ezekiel 40–48. It is not certain whether these chapters embody Ezekiel's own hope or were composed by a later, anonymous writer. However, as the book stands now, the vision of the future return of Yahweh's glory parallels the vision of its present departure. There is no indication elsewhere in the book that the glory, and all it signifies, are to be manifest and available to the remnant of Israel in the time between the times.

The glory of Yahweh and the presence of Yahweh are not identical, but they are closely related. God is present everywhere, sustaining all creation. The glory of God is also everywhere, to those who have eyes to see. The glory is a manifestation of the presence which provides the conditions of existence, always and everywhere. The presence is the source of vitality, strength, wisdom, love, blessing. These are available to everyone, everywhere, always. However, many in ancient Israel did not understand this. For them God—the God of the fathers, the God of the covenant, the God they had known—was present and accessible primarily, if not exclusively, in the land of Israel, in the city of David, in the temple of Jerusalem. Even the Book of Ezekiel, with its visions of the departure and return of the glory of Yahweh, implies that the effective presence of God is tied to a properly functioning and purified holy place. God is Lord of all nations and peoples, but God's saving presence, the special power of the blessing, is made available through the worship of Yahweh in Yahweh's chosen place. Nor is this conviction merely an ancient or priestly phenomenon, it is the conviction of many religious people today. For them the forms of worship have changed, but the fundamental understanding of the means of access to the saving power of God has not.

Jeremiah had a correcting word to say about such an understanding in a letter he sent from Jerusalem to Judean exiles in Babylon sometime after the first deportation in 597 B.C. The text is Jer 29:1-14. There is nothing like this letter anywhere else in the prophetic corpus. This alone would mark it as a special prophetic text. However, its chief importance lies in its content. The historical setting is clearly described in the introduction (29:1-3). Prophets like Hananiah in Jerusalem, and others among the exiles in Babylon, were predicting a speedy restoration to their homeland and the removal of the yoke of Babylonian rule (27:16–28:16). Jeremiah disputed this and insisted that the nation would sink deeper into subjugation and that the time of captivity would be very long. This conflict in prophetic judgment is the subject of chaps. 27–29, which constitute a small booklet within the larger Jeremianic collection.

The course of events confirmed Jeremiah's prophecy of a long captivity. This may be one reason why these words were preserved. However, fulfillment alone does not establish the value of a prophetic word; it is the substance that matters most. The enduring word that emerged from Jeremiah's dispute with the other prophet is contained in this letter, and it is one of his most important contributions to the prophetic witness of faith.

Jeremiah's counsel to the exiles was threefold: First, they could expect to spend the rest of their lives in Babylon, so they should seek their welfare and happiness there. Second, they should seek the welfare of the people among whom they were living, because their own well-being was inseparable from that of the people among whom they lived. Third, they should seek God right where they were, and not long to return to Jerusalem, for God was accessible wherever they happened to be.

These were radical words in Judea in the sixth century B.C. The kingdom was in process of being destroyed. The royal line of David, which Judeans had believed would last forever (2 Samuel 7), was threatened with annihilation. The people's possession of the land of promise had already been drastically reduced and stood in final jeopardy. The very survival of the people of the covenant was in serious doubt. In the face of this enormous national trauma and a totally uncertain future, Jeremiah calmly delivered his advice. There are two questions to be answered here.

The first is raised by Jeremiah's instruction to the exiles to marry (v 6). Did he intend this to mean marriage with non-Israelites? The letter does not say. Does this silence imply that intermarriage was acceptable to Jeremiah? Naturally, we cannot be certain, but Jeremiah's instruction does not preclude intermarriage, and therefore, it may be legitimate to infer that this possibility was within the purview of his prophetic teaching. The issue is important for it concerns the openness of the covenantal community and the conditions of membership within it.

We do not have space to discuss the history of this issue in ancient Israel, and the literary evidence is fragmentary and difficult to interpret. All we can do here is call attention to this important question posed by Jeremiah's letter to the exiles. The issue is not merely historical, it confronts every religious community. Who may belong to the religious group? What are the conditions of membership? How should the religious community interact with the world around it? Should it be self-protective and exclusive? Should it be passively open to those who seek membership? Should it be aggressive in the recruitment of new participants? These questions came to occupy Judaism in the years after Jeremiah. His letter to the exiles does not anticipate them, let alone provide solutions for them. However, the liberal spirit that animates it suggests openness to the world rather than parochialism.

The second question arises over the time indicated in Jer 29:12-13. Several versions translate v 12 in such a way that the seeking and finding of God in Babylon are placed at the end of the period of exile, on the eve of restoration to the land of Judah. "Then when you call to me, and come to plead with me I will listen to you" (JB; cf. CBAT, NASV, TEV, NIV, and RSV). Others, however, render the verse so that it makes the time of reference indeterminate, saying in effect, "Whenever

you call to me and come to plead with me, I will listen to you"
(cf. NEB, NAB, and NJV). The Hebrew conjunction is the
multipurpose *waw,* which can mean many things, depending
upon the context. The second, indefinite, temporal reference
seems to be meant here. Had the writer wished to place the
exiles' seeking and finding God specifically in the time of
restoration, and not before, he could have done so without any
ambiguity by using one of the common Hebrew words for
"then" or "at that time." However, the writer left the
statement indefinite. It seems to me, therefore, that we may
understand Jeremiah's word to be that whenever and wherever
they sought God with all their hearts, God would be found by
them, would hear their prayers, and would respond to their
deepest needs. If this is indeed what vv 12-13 say, then the
meaning for faithful people in all generations is clear.

Jeremiah's counsel to the exiles to seek the welfare of the
people in the cities where they found themselves is unambi-
guously stated, and this too is a radical word, not only for
Jeremiah's contemporaries, but for people in all times and
places. It goes against our natural instincts, our cultural
conditioning, and our personal preferences. The implications
for our religious, social, and political attitudes and behavior are
extensive and profound.

We began this chapter with a discussion of Jer 7:1-15. In that
famous speech, delivered in the temple of Jerusalem, the
prophet warned the Judean worshipers against a superstitious
trust in the temple as a guarantee of the protection and support
of God. He also suggested that divine blessing was linked to the
people's righteousness. In defining the behavior acceptable to
God, he referred to several of the Ten Commandments (7:9)
and to the ancient ideal of protection for the resident alien, the
orphan, and the widow (v 6). He placed the fulfillment of these
moral goals above ritual performance as a response to the
claims of God.

Other oracles in the books of the prophets are devastating in
their criticism of Israel's worship. Among these are Isa 1:10-17;

Amos 5:21-27; and Hos 5:1-7; 10:1-8. Some of these words appear to constitute a total rejection of ritual as a legitimate service of God. Some biblical scholars have understood them in this way and have set the prophetic tradition of the OT over against the priestly as incompatible rivals. Other scholars have rejected this interpretation of the oracles, arguing that the prophets rejected, not ritual itself, but ritualism unaccompanied by zeal for social justice and moral integrity. Others have concluded that the prophets rejected the ancient system of animal sacrifice. In this view, other forms of worship, e.g., singing, praying, and professing the saving acts of God, were acceptable to the prophets. In these last two interpretations, what seems to be a radical rejection of worship in the prophetic oracles is regarded as a rhetorical exaggeration. Presumably, this exaggeration is rooted in passionate indignation over ritual abuses, and its purpose is to create the strongest possible impression upon the hearers. The interpretation dominating biblical criticism today is that the prophets condemned ritual abuses as well as ritualism unaccompanied by righteousness.

• Whether or not this view is correct, the prophetic criticism of worship is pertinent to religious life in the twentieth century. The prophetic word challenges believers in all generations to consider seriously what they are doing in public worship and personal devotion. The prophetic words probe, challenge, provoke, and stimulate greater self-awareness and greater responsibility on the part of religious people. The questions raised are relevant to every worshiping congregation. Although the forms of worship today differ in many respects from those of ancient Israel, the reasons why people worship, and their experiences in doing so, are similar. There is continuity between Israel's worship and our own. Our worship is subject to many of the same abuses the prophets criticized, and Israel's worship had many of the same strengths that can be recognized in present-day worship. Indeed, most of these strengths are a legacy from ancient Israel.

Prophetic teaching concerning the worship of God reaches its climax in the great concluding poem of Isaiah 40–55. This poem comprises the whole of Isaiah 55. Here is a lyrical prophecy of the eschatological celebration of the presence and word of God. No ordinary sanctuary is mentioned, for the worshipers are "everyone who thirsts," that is, all humanity.

In the introduction to his proclamation of the new age of salvation, the writer of Isaiah 40–55 emphasized the word of God, which would stand forever amid everything transient and human (40:6-8), and the glory of God, which would ultimately be made manifest to all humanity (v 5). In the concluding scene of the drama of salvation, the writer lays stress upon the word of God (55:10-11). The glory is not mentioned explicitly; however, it is implicit in the entire scene. The glory symbolizes the presence and power of God, and these are to be found by those who heed the prophet's injunction to "seek the Lord" (v 6).

In the eschatological banquet, which culminates not only all institutions of worship, but all of life itself, Israel's special knowledge of God becomes the common blessing of all nations (vv 4-5). In this way the purpose of creation is fulfilled, so that the very mountains, hills, and trees can be said to take part in the acknowledgement of the Creator (v 12). The satisfaction of the deepest human needs and the fulfillment of life are free gifts of God (vv 1-2). They cannot be earned. However, moral earnestness is a part of any true response to the grace of God. Repentance and acceptance of God's forgiveness characterize those who know and seek the Lord (vv 6-7). Thus the ethical teaching of the prophetic forerunners of this anonymous exilic writer is taken up into his lyric evocation of the culmination of the story of God and Israel.

# IV. THE RIGHTEOUSNESS OF GOD

Most of the prophetic writings could be treated under the heading we have chosen for this chapter. The theme comprehends the proclamation of God's judgment on both the individual and the nation and the affirmation of God's righteous demand—the righteousness of human beings in response to the righteousness of God. It also includes the mercy of God and the corresponding requirement of mercy and compassion in people. Both justice and mercy are aspects of the righteousness of God, and this righteousness is grounded in love. The entire story of God and Israel may be told and interpreted under this heading. In order to explicate the theme fully as it appears in the books of the prophets we would have to give a full account of these books, which, of course, is not possible here. We must be highly selective of the kinds of writing and of the themes contained in them, and so we have chosen: Jer 11:1-13 (covenant, judgment, idolatry); Isa 2:12-22 (the day of wrath); Ezekiel 18 (individual responsibility—punishment and forgiveness); Isa 10:5-21 (Assyria as the instrument of God's punishment of Israel); Isa 19:16-26 (the conversion of Egypt and Assyria to faith in God); Hosea 2 (the story of God and

Israel); Jer 12:1-3 (the problem of prosperity of the wicked); Isa 11:1-9 (the righteous ruler, the vicegerent of God); and Jer 31:31-34 (the new covenant). Most of the themes of prophetic teaching are contained in these passages: history and eschatology, the providence of God, the rule of God, social justice, individual morality and retribution, covenant, the wrath of God, the love of God, wealth and poverty, power and weakness, order and freedom, international justice and peace, blessing and affliction, suffering and death, sin and repentance. We will begin with the sermon on the covenant in Jeremiah 11, and conclude with the famous prophecy of the new covenant in Jeremiah 31.

### Jeremiah and the Covenant (Jeremiah 11)

The covenant speech in Jer 11:1-13 is one of a substantial number of sermonic discourses in prose which make up one of the principal strata of the book. The literary style, as well as the theological emphases, are similar to those of the great sermonic introduction to the book of Deuteronomy (chaps. 5–11). Jeremiah 11, like the other prose sermons in the book, may reflect an oracle originally delivered by Jeremiah; however, in its present form it appears to be a product of a group of anonymous exilic and postexilic writers who composed or edited much of the material in the books of Deuteronomy, 1 and 2 Kings, and parts of Joshua, Judges, and 1 and 2 Samuel. The teaching of this so-called Deuteronomic (or Deuteronomistic) school has close affinities with the message of the preexilic prophets. However, the covenant plays a more explicit role in this literature than in the oracles of the prophets. Moreover, a much smaller number of theological motifs is contained in this material, and they are treated in a much more uniform manner. The style is didactic and repetitive, material appropriate for use in teaching or preaching. It seems reasonable to surmise that it was developed among congregations of Jewish exiles after the destruction of the monarchy.

These sermons lack the rich imagery and rhetorical power of the poetic oracles of the prophets. Few of the lines are truly memorable, and the theology tends to be simplistic and legalistic. In this regard it stands in tension with other prophetic writings. Nevertheless, these prose sermons deserve our attention for they represent a new form of religious literature which is the direct forerunner of the modern sermon. All preachers today stand in debt to the Deuteronomic writers of the sixth century. In addition to their value for understanding the history of OT literature and religion, the prose sermons of Jeremiah have a continuing didactic value for modern congregations.

The message of Jer 11:1-13 is straightforward. God entered into covenant with Israel at the time of their deliverance from slavery in Egypt. This covenant required Israel to obey the commandments of God, and in return God renewed the promise to give them the land of Canaan, which had originally been promised to their ancestors. Despite perennial warnings, Israel refused to be obedient. Therefore, a series of curses, contained in the covenant, were put into effect, but this failed to bring about Israel's obedience. As a result the supreme curse would fall upon Israel, namely, dispossession of the land of promise. This would be a punishment long deserved.

There are other prose sermons in the Book of Jeremiah (e.g., 7:1–8:6; 18:1-12; 21:1-10; 25:1-11; 34:8-22; 35:1-19; and 44:1-14), and their message is similar. It is uncertain whether these sermons were written originally for a preexilic audience or an exilic one. Since the theology of these passages is in essential agreement with that of the poetic oracles many scholars regard them as Jeremiah's, though actually written by his scribe Baruch. Other scholars believe they were written later for Jews in exile by an anonymous disciple or disciples of Jeremiah. They base this conviction on the differences in style and theological emphasis between the prose sermons and the poetic oracles.

Interpreters should take account of both of these possibilities. Addressed to a preexilic audience, the sermons would seem to have been intended to elicit repentance and amendment of life. Addressed to an exilic audience, they would have served well to justify the fall of Judah as a righteous act of God and to warn the exiles not to repeat the sins of the past. We know that these and the other writings in the book were collected and transmitted in the exile, since they tell the story of Jeremiah up to that time. Therefore, whether or not they were first intended for a preexilic audience, they were intended eventually for the exiles and other survivors of the fall of Judah. For these people the sermons, as well as other portions of the book, would have helped strengthen their faith by explaining the fall as a manifestation of God's justice rather than a defeat of God's power by the gods of a foreign nation. They would also have encouraged the exiles to order their lives so as to avoid a similar punishment in the future.

A rapid reading of the recent English versions shows no serious problems of translation in Jer 11:1-13. This text is clear, expansive prose in which the meaning lies open, on the surface, as it were. It is quite different from the compact, subtly nuanced poetry of some oracles in the book.

● Using the message of this text in the setting of modern life is not so straightforward as translating the ancient Hebrew into modern English. There are pitfalls along the way. Modern interpreters should move slowly in trying to formulate general religious truths from this text, because it deals concretely with the history of a particular people. In this passage the writer declared to the people of Judah that they would be dispossessed from their land because of their perennial and incorrigible disobedience to God's commandments. This is not the formulation of a universal moral truth, but an analysis of their distinctive history. Is there then a general truth lying beneath the surface that we can uncover and appropriate for the instruction in our own time?

The temptation for interpreters in the United States is to apply the prophetic analysis to their own nation. There is a long and pervasive tradition in American culture that this is the promised land of the modern era and that the American nation is the new Israel of God. There must be some analogy between the experience of ancient Israel and the experience of the United States, or this conviction could not have arisen and persisted so long. Nevertheless, the differences between the two nations are far greater than the similarities. Indeed, socially, politically, economically, and technologically the United States is totally unlike ancient Israel, which was a small, homogeneous nation with an agricultural and pastoral economy, little military power and no capacity to influence the cultures and nations of the ancient world. The contrast with the United States is obvious. Again, in Israel no distinction was made among the religious, social, and political orders. Separation of church and state—even the *idea* of separation of church and state—was inconceivable, and so was the notion of individual religious liberty. In the light of these innumerable differences, we should be cautious about drawing parallels between Israel's religious situation and our own.

We have suggested that the audience for whom Jer 11:1-13 was ultimately intended was the survivors of the fall of Judah and that its purpose was to strengthen their faith in God's righteous providence and encourage them to learn from the experience of preexilic Israel. If this analysis is correct then it may help us to appropriate Jeremiah's covenant-speech for ourselves. Perhaps we should place ourselves with the Judean exiles and ask, What are the consequences for our faith and for our understanding of the nature of religious community of the fall of Judah, as this event was interpreted by the prophets. Perhaps a lesson to be drawn is that the people of the covenant are not to be identified with a national state. Perhaps the mistake of the ancient Israelite community was trying to become like the nations, possessing territory with definable boundaries and being ruled by a king. Perhaps now the effort to become like the nations was at an end, and, in the providence of God, Israel was meant to understand herself in different terms. Should we not then, as heirs of the biblical tradition, identify our covenantal community, not with Israel under the monarchy, but with Israel in exile? If the covenantal community is to be distinguished from all political entities—and this, it seems to me, is the outcome of prophetic teaching—then we should observe this distinction in proclaiming the demands of God and interpreting the fortunes of the various communities to which we belong.

## The Day of Wrath (Isaiah 2)

We move from pedestrian prose to the exalted poetry of Isa 2:6-22. There are a few minor problems of translation in this passage, but they do not affect the meaning of the whole. The issue in choosing among recent versions of this text is not how to deal with the minor textual uncertainties but how to convey the dramatic force of the poetry. In my judgment, CBAT and RSV do this very well, NASB does it poorly, and TEV not at all. TEV renders the passage as prose! It also paraphrases here, as elsewhere, and thus blunts the impact of this magnificent poem. The other versions are adequate poetically but are not equal to RSV and CBAT. For example, the Hebrew of vv 12-16 uses the preposition "against" ten times, creating a mounting staccato effect that is devastating. RSV and CBAT capture this effect, but NEB and NIV lose it by translating the preposition as "for" instead of "against." Again, v 22 is very important in the development of the mood of the poem. After the fury of what goes before, there is a lull, and then comes the single line of the conclusion: "Turn away from man / in whose nostrils is breath, / for of what account is he?" (RSV). CBAT is equally good in capturing the effect of this conclusion, but the other versions are less successful.

A high percentage of the oracles of the preexilic prophets contain accusations of human evil and announcements of divine judgment. Indeed, there are so many oracles of judgment in the books of the prophets that they blend together when read rapidly, and the impression they create obscures other features of the literature. To be appreciated fully, the oracles should be read slowly, a few at a time. Many of them, like Isa 2:6-22, merit reading again and again. They should be read aloud for the poetry to have its full effect. But interpretations of masterful poems pale beside the originals, and there is no substitute for the poem itself. Isaiah 2 is not so much a text from which to extract theological ideas as a work of art to be perceived.

The poem is all about human arrogance. It depicts the vainglorious pride of human beings, trying to master the world and control their destinies by their own wisdom and power. Their efforts include both politics and religion. In the end, however, they are all futile. Such mastery and control are simply not given to humankind. They belong only to God. Here we see the awe which Isaiah experienced before God in his inaugural vision (Isaiah 6) translated into a picture of terror before the wrath of God. For Isaiah, God was first of all the transcendent, Holy One, before whom one falls in reverence and humility. Therefore pride and idolatry, which characterize much human behavior, are totally at odds with the fundamental conditions of human existence before God. The inevitable outcome of all human efforts to achieve autonomy and mastery of the world is humiliation and destruction. This is not a pretty picture, but it is unforgettable.

Isaiah's poem is undated, and therefore we cannot place it in relation to any of the specific historical events of his time. We do not know, e.g., whether he composed it in a time of peace, prosperity, and political strength for the nation of Judah, or in a time of adversity, or even disaster. Probably it doesn't matter.

• This poem is not merely a commentary on the affairs of particular people in a particular time and place. It can serve as a commentary on all human behavior. The pretentions and idolatries of Judah alluded to in this poem can be matched by similar attitudes and activities in the lives of people in all times and places. Nor should we think of Isaiah's awesome picture of the wrath of God as pointing to the end of history, the eschaton, the final judgment. This is not an apocalpytic vision of the age to come, but a prophetic account of the present age. This is what happens to the proud! However, we miss Isaiah's point if we take his poem merely as a description of what happens in human history. His point is that this is what *ought* to happen! This is what the arrogance and idolatry of human beings deserve. The reasons we deserve it, of course, is that in behaving this way we usurp the power and authority of God. Isaiah was not merely describing the course of history realistically; he was interpreting it theologically. Only in the light of faith in a sovereign God could one condemn human pride as Isaiah did in this oracle. If "man is the measure of all things," a judgment like Isaiah's is unreasonable and unfair. It is only on the basis of faith in God that such a statement makes sense.

This oracle is easy to apply to our own times. Isaiah's picture of the destructive consequences of human pride and idolatry has been fulfilled more terribly in our century than in any other in human history. The challenge of this passage to the modern reader is not in deciding whether this is really what happens in human life, but in judging whether the faith in God to which it points is true.

### Individual Responsibility and Reward (Ezekiel 18)

We turn next to an entirely different kind of text. This prophetic treatise (Ezekiel 18), which is not an oracle in the conventional sense, is wholly concerned with individual retribution. Do individual human beings get what they deserve from the hand of God, and are they free at a given moment to earn their own reward or punishment?

Ezekiel's essay was provoked by a popular complaint that the current generation in Israel was suffering because of the sins of their fathers. The complaint was expressed in a proverb: "The fathers have eaten sour grapes, and the children's teeth are set on edge" (v 2). The same proverb is quoted in Jer 31:29, so it seems to have been repeated widely during and after the period of Judah's national demise. Since there is no indication of literary dependence between Jeremiah and Ezekiel at this point, we may assume that each writer heard the proverb himself and made his own response to it. Jeremiah's response is very brief. It is that in the time to come the people will not repeat the proverb, for then individuals will be punished for their own sins and not for those of their fathers. In making this assertion Jeremiah seems to concede that in his own age the children were indeed suffering for the sins of the parents. Whether he was right about this, and whether the same thing is true of people in other times and places, are issues to which we shall return, but first we will consider Ezekiel's response to the proverb.

He said it wasn't true! To make his point as clear as possible he told a parable about three men, father, son, and grandson. The first is a righteous man, and as a consequence of his righteousness he lives (vv 5-9). This man's son does not live up to his father's standards, but commits evil. As a result he dies (vv 10-13). However, the second man's son avoids the evil of his father and is entirely righteous, like his grandfather. As a result he lives (vv 14-17). The second man is not granted life automatically because his father was a righteous man; rather, because he himself is wicked, he dies. However, the third man does not die because of his father's wickedness, but because of his own righteousness he lives. Thus, contrary to the popular proverb, one generation does not suffer because of the sins of another, nor is one generation rewarded because of the virtues of another. There is no carryover of reward and punishment from one generation to the next. Each generation—each individual—lives or dies as a result of its own righteousness or iniquity. But this is not all.

Not only is one's living or dying not determined by the behavior of the father, but it is not even determined irrevocably by one's own previous behavior. If a wicked man turns from his wickedness and lives righteously, he will live (vv 21-23), and if a righteous man turns from his virtue and sins, he will die (v 24).

Is this analysis universally correct? Children really do suffer for the sins of their parents. The attitudes and behavior of one generation deeply affect the lives of the next generation, and, to a diminishing extent, the generations after that. When the attitudes are widespread, and especially if they are institutionalized in the structures of society, their effects may persist for centuries. Both in families and in societies, it is an empirical fact that when the fathers eat sour grapes the children's teeth are set on edge. Since Ezekiel 18 denies this, must we then reject it as a rationalistic fantasy of an unreal world?

There are two principal clues to guide our understanding and appreciation of this text, one external, and the other internal. The external clue is the proverb which the prophet quotes, and the internal one is the recurring reference to living and dying within the treatise itself.

The proverb, "The fathers have eaten sour grapes and the children's teeth are set on edge," excused Ezekiel's generation of responsibility for the fall of Judah and blamed previous generations. Ezekiel's treatise can be taken as an effort to counteract this attitude of irresponsibility. Understood in this way, his response is something we can affirm. The moral lethargy reflected in the proverb was a deterrent to the recovery of the Jewish community from the effects of the fall of Judah, and it was incompatible with prophetic teaching. Ezekiel's response to the proverb was, in effect, to tell the generation of the Exile that whether they lived or died depended upon themselves and not upon the legacy they had received from the past. Ezekiel did not suggest in his essay what forms the exiles' life might take, or what the limits and conditions of their social and economic achievements might be. He did not promise them complete mastery over their destiny, nor did he deny the existence of continuing problems resulting from the fall of the Kingdom of Judah. He told his contemporaries simply—and this is the internal clue to our appreciation—that upright people "live" and wicked people "die." Thus he invited his hearers to choose between life and death.

Life and death are not defined in this parabolic essay. The silence of the text in this regard means that, on the one hand, we can only speculate about the sense Ezekiel intended these terms to have, and, on the other hand, we are free to attach our own sense to them, in the light of our own knowledge of life and of the broader biblical witness of faith. Ezekiel's parable of the three generations invites us to engage in this kind of reflection.

Living and dying in this passage cannot be merely physical. If this were the case, it would be impossible for a wicked man to turn from evil and live (vv 21-22), for he would already have died as a result of his wickedness (vv 10-13). If one can die as a result of one's wickedness and then turn from that wickedness and live, then the living and dying are not simply physical, they must be something more—or less—than these. "To live" here must signify a range of positive experiences, conditions, and relationships, and "to die" must signify a corresponding range of negative possibilities. These possibilities need not be merely "spiritual," in the usual sense of that term. They might also be tangible. For example, they might include health and disease or prosperity and poverty. However, they would certainly include inward possibilities—mental, psychological, emotional, spiritual.

Ezekiel presented his parable as the word of God. Throughout, it is God who speaks. Thus, what the prophet was discussing first of all was God's reaction to righteousness and wickedness, rather than the tangible consequences of the two. He was declaring that in the sight of God the upright person lives and the evil person dies. This does not mean that such living and dying take place only in the sight of God, independently of the outward course of life. Ultimately, the two realms must be the same. However, to assert that something is right or wrong in the sight of God is to make a declaration concerning its intrinsic worth, apart from its outward appearance. If the assertions made in Ezekiel 18 are taken in this way, they are reasonable when judged in relation to actual human experience.

● The subject of Jeremiah 11 was Israel's covenant. The subject of Ezekiel 18 is "a man." What is said about the first may not be applicable to people in other times and places. However, what is said about the second would appear to be applicable to anyone, regardless of time and place. The covenant is an aspect of the life of a particular nation during a particular period of its history. The facts of that case, and the truths that might be deduced from them, may have little or no bearing upon modern life. In order to apply the teaching to our own situation, we would need to establish the factors common to our situation and Israel's. The responsiblity of the interpreter is different in the case of Ezekiel 18. Here the writer presents a theory concerning individual moral retribution that is not tied to the history of Israel or the distinctive features of the nation's corporate life. As stated, the text appears to apply to every human life. Therefore the modern interpreter is justified in asking whether and to what extent the theory provides a true account of human experience, without first having to establish the cultural links between the writer's setting and our own. Upon close examination we may find in the writer's treatment of the subject evidence of cultural conditioning. We may conclude that there are specifically Israelite features in the language, imagery, or presuppositions of the text. We will certainly notice that the examples of righteous and wicked behavior are based upon the moral standards of the Israelite covenant, esp. the Ten Commandments. Nevertheless, the text is not merely about what happens to Israelites, but what happens to human beings.

If Ezekiel was trying to combat defeatism among his exilic contemporaries, as we have suggested, his treatise on individual retribution has considerable cogency. It minimizes the influence that one's ancestors have upon one's own life, and in this respect, it simplifies human experience. Still, it makes several points worthy of consideration. It declares that one's future is never completely blocked by the legacy of the past—that, in the providence of God, there are always possibilities of new beginning. One really can make a fresh start. It also declares that one is not responsible for the sins and failures of one's parents, nor for their virtues and achievements. One "lives" or "dies," in the sense that really matters, as a result of one's own life-enhancing or life-destroying deeds. According to Ezekiel, things work out this way because this is the way God wills human existence to be. However, if he has described human affairs accurately—if this is the way life really is—then one does not have to share Ezekiel's faith in God in order to agree with his analysis of the human situation. One can disagree with him over the reason why life is this way, and still agree with him in his description of it.

On the other hand, if the life and death about which Ezekiel is speaking are religious, or spiritual, either wholly or in part, then one would not be able to agree with his analysis, or appropriate it meaningfully into one's own life, without sharing his faith. If the reward of virtue is knowing that one is righteous and acceptable in God's sight, and the punishment of iniquity is knowing that one is sinful and unacceptable in God's sight, then attaining such knowledge is impossible apart from an active faith in God. This appears to be the ultimate implication of the essay. We could translate this affirmation into nontheological terms, by asserting that righteousness is its own reward and wickedness its own punishment, but we would lose an important dimension of Ezekiel's statement in doing so. This would be to equate God with the moral order, or the laws of human behavior. However, the God whom Ezekiel talks about and presupposes in all his writings is personal, and not merely an aspect of the natural order.

## The Prosperity of the Wicked (Jeremiah 12)

According to Ezekiel 18, the righteous live and the wicked die. According to the next text we are to consider, Jer 12:1-3, the wicked often prosper. What shall we make of this contrary assertion?

Jer 12:1-3 stands in the middle of one of the prophet's complaints (11:18–12:6). These verses state the general theological problem suggested by the attempted murder of a man of God: Why do the wicked prosper? Jeremiah had given up all private interests in order to dedicate himself completely to God's cause. Although his proclamation contained severe moral criticism of the people of Judah and warnings of national calamity, it was ultimately directed at the people's good. Therefore, the violent response he received from them perplexed him and led him to doubt the justice of God. Are human affairs ordered by a righteous providence when the godly suffer persecution and the godless thrive? This question is asked repeatedly in the OT. It is the theme of Psalm 73, e.g., and it is one of the dominant motifs of the Book of Job. The prophet Habakkuk was another who joined Jeremiah in his complaint to God (Hab 1:1-4). The answer given by the psalmist is that the wicked eventually receive their just punishment, even though they seem to prosper in the short run. Jeremiah, Habakkuk, and the writer of the Book of Job do not propose any theoretical solution to the problem. The practical solution that Jeremiah adopted himself was to turn from his questioning of God and redouble his efforts as a prophet (Jer 12:5; 15:19-21). The absence of a theoretical answer sets a limit to our responsibility as interpreters. We have before us a major theological question and no answer.

Jer 12:1-6 resembles Jer 31:29-30 (the proverb about the sour grapes) in posing a profound theological question and providing no theoretical answer. To the charge that children suffer for the sins of their parents (31:29), a charge that challenges the justice of God, the only answer is that it will not always be so (v 30). Similarly, when the question arises in Jeremiah's mind concerning the prosperity of the wicked (12:1), he does not formulate a theoretical answer. His response is not theological but practical. He carries on his prophetic ministry, perplexed by the mystery of God's providence, but not immobilized by it.

No guidelines are laid down in the books of the prophets to help us resolve the problems that arise when we place texts like Jer 12:1-3 and Ezekiel 18 side by side. The questions and the contradiction in perspectives they seem to exhibit must be dealt with according to canons of understanding that lie outside the prophetic works themselves. Two principal solutions to the problem of the prosperity of the wicked have been proposed by interpreters of the Bible. The first is to deny that the wicked really prosper, at least in the sense that matters most, namely, psychological and spiritual well-being. This answer to the question may be supported by an appeal to Ezekiel 18, if living and dying there mean inward states of being rather than material conditions. The second principal solution is to project the resolution of the problem into a future time. We have already referred to Psalm 73 where the writer affirms that the wicked will eventually receive their punishment. The implication is that this will take place within their lifetime. Other biblical writers, and a great many later Jews and Christians, expected the final working out of justice to occur in a future age or an afterlife. These ideas, however, carry us beyond the immediate tasks of interpreting prophetic texts.

## God and Israel (Hosea 2)

The OT prophets believed that all the kingdoms of the earth were subject to the righteous rule of God. They gave primary attention to the nation of Israel, but they published many oracles concerning foreign nations as well. Each of the four major collections of prophetic writings contains a substantial body of material dealing with foreign nations. There are large blocks of oracles concerning foreign nations in Isaiah, Jeremiah, and Ezekiel (Isaiah 13–23; Jeremiah 46–51; and Ezekiel 25–32), and several parts of The Book of the Twelve Prophets as well (Amos 1:3–2:5; Joel 3:1–21; Obadiah; Jonah;

Nahum; Zeph 2:4-7; Zech 9:1-8, 14:1-21). In addition there are innumerable allusions and brief oracular statements concerning foreign nations scattered throughout the books of the prophets. This is a considerable body of literature. Obviously, it had an important place in the prophetic tradition and in the formation of the biblical canon. Nevertheless, it is almost totally neglected in modern teaching of the Bible.

This modern neglect of the oracles concerning non-Israelite nations is not entirely undeserved. Compared to the oracles concerning Israel, they are monotonous and two-dimensional. Many of them ring the changes on a single theme: sooner or later in the justice of God, the nations will be punished for their pride, their idolatry, and their oppression of weaker peoples. This is an important theme of prophetic theology, but it becomes tedious when repeated over and over again. Furthermore, there is little if anything among these oracles that is edifying to individual persons concerning their relationship to God or concerning other important issues in their lives. On the other hand, they do merit some attention, if for no other reason than that they raise for us the important theological question about the rule of God in world history.

In our discussion we will consider briefly two oracles concerning foreign nations from the Book of Isaiah (10:5-21 and 19:16-25). First, however, we will examine Hosea 2, which presents a theological interpretation of Israel's history.

Here is one of the most interesting passages in the prophetic canon, and it is one of the most important theologically. In it the prophet interprets the history of Israel as a marriage between God and the covenant people. The marriage began when God led Israel out of slavery in Egypt and brought her into the land of Canaan (vv 14-15). The fruits of this land, which supported her life, were gifts of God. However, she did not remain faithful to God, but pursued "lovers." These were the deities of Canaan. Devotion to a religion of nature undermined her faith and corrupted her morality. These consequences are referred to only metaphorically in chap. 2; however, they are catalogued in detail in the oracles in chaps. 4–13. Israel interpreted the fruits of the earth as gifts of the gods of the earth (v 5) and proved to be incorrigible in her apostasy. Therefore, Yahweh would devastate the land and exile Israel from it, not only as a punishment, but also as a disciplinary measure aimed at bringing about her repentance and a renewal of her fidelity to the true God (vv 10-17). Once this had taken place God would renew the marriage covenant with Israel, restore her to the land she required as the basis of life, and fulfill her corporate life in righteousness (vv 18-23).

A similar interpretation of Israel's history is made in Hosea 11. However, there the metaphor used to symbolize God's relationship with Israel is that of parent and child, rather than husband and wife. The marriage metaphor is used again in Hosea's report of his call to prophesy (1:2-3), and in the narrative about his redemption of his profligate wife (3:1-5). Thus, the two family metaphors—marriage and parenthood—are central to Hosea's proclamation.

There are many details that we would want to examine here if we were doing a thorough exegesis of the chapter. We would want to determine as far as possible what historical events are alluded to, and how these allusions relate to what we know about the history of Israel from other sources. We would find that the picture presented here conforms to the broad outline of the story of Israel contained in the Pentateuch and Former Prophets (Joshua to 2 Kings). However, the real significance of Hosea 2 lies, not in its recounting of the history of Israel, but in the theological interpretation of this history. The first question for the interpreter to ask, then, is whether Hosea's allegory of Israel as the wife of Yahweh is a valid representation of Israel's experience.

There are two ways to affirm Hosea's interpretation of Israel's history. The first involves a merely historical judgment, while the second requires a judgment of faith. As historians of culture we can evaluate the place of religion in Israel's life. If Israel came into being, as the biblical sources indicate, as a people defined by a religious covenant, then the quality of her life and her existence as a nation were bound up with the strength and integrity of the religious commitment of her people. The structures of Israel's corporate life, the self-understanding of individual Israelites, the quality of human relations within Israelite society, the economic and political values of the people, in short, the whole of Israelite life and culture, was an expression of her faith in God. When her faith was eroded by religious syncretism or idolatry, her social unity and moral strength were undermined, and she became vulnerable to deliberate or unwitting assimilation by other nations.

If Israel came into being as the people of Yahweh, then she could not surrender her faith in Yahweh, and the understanding of human existence that was rooted in that faith, without becoming a different sort of people or ceasing to be a people at all. If this is what Hosea was saying, we can accept his analysis as historically accurate. Moreover, our acceptance does not require us to share his faith. However, when we ask whether Hosea's story of Israel is true theologically, we cannot answer the question on the basis of historical considerations alone. To interpret the creation of the Israelite nation and its settlement of the land of Canaan as blessings of God, and the dissolution of the nation as a punishment of God, is an act of faith, not of historiography. Furthermore, there is no way to move by rational argument from historiography to faith. One can perceive the hand of God in history only because of prior conviction.

Why did Hosea tell the story of Israel as an allegory of an adulterous wife? Surely it could not have been because the ingredients of Israel's history suggested it. It must have been because of the nature of Hosea's own religious experience. His knowledge of God must have been such that he found it appropriate to talk about the relationship of Israel to God as that of a wife to her husband (or in the case of chap. 11, that of a child to its parent). This does not mean that Hosea's knowledge of God was unique in Israel, or that he was the first to speak about the relationship to God in personal terms. On the contrary, God is represented as personal in all the OT traditions, and the relationship of God to human beings is spoken of everywhere in metaphors drawn from social institutions and social relations, e.g., judge, king, warrior, shepherd, teacher, and parent. Hosea did not invent this kind of language about God. What he did was to give a new emphasis to the familial metaphors of marriage and parenthood by creating the allegorical poems of chaps. 2 and 11, and by performing the prophetic acts with his wife and children that are reported in chaps. 1 and 3.

The images of God as husband and parent, so unforgettably embodied by Hosea in his allegories, connote a wider scope and greater depth in the divine-human relationship than any other metaphors employed in the OT. The range of involvement and the limit of responsibility between king and subject, judge and petitioner, captain and soldier, or teacher and pupil, e.g., are relatively narrow, and the depth of feeling between them is correspondingly shallow. By contrast, the range of involvement and responsibility in a husband-wife or parent-child relationship is unlimited, and the depth of feeling is extreme. Furthermore, these relationships are lifelong, whereas the others are usually transient or sporadic. Thus the images drawn from the family comprehend the whole of life throughout its length. For this reason they are superior theologically to images taken from other kinds of social relationship.

When we move from the situation of Hosea in the eighth century B.C. to our own, it is difficult to translate his analysis of Israel's history into one that applies to our own nation or to other modern communities. Taken as a whole, the story of ancient Israel is unique. It is not at all like our story, however we may define ourselves sociologically. But the metaphors of marriage and parenthood are transferrable to our own experience, with all that these metaphors imply about the relationship of human beings to God.

• The metaphor of marriage used in chap. 2 casts God in a masculine role. In this respect Hosea's language is characteristic of the OT generally, where language about God was conditioned by Israel's patriarchal society and her male-dominated culture. Hosea 11 is somewhat different, however. Although we may presume that Hosea was thinking paternally when he composed this oracle, the imagery he actually employed is not distinctively so. It applies as well to mothers, and thus it seems legitimate to refer to God as parent rather than father when interpreting this passage, and this usage is certainly more adequate theologically in our own time. Modern readers who insist upon viewing the figure of God in Hosea 11 as a father should at least take note of the loving tenderness which characterizes God there, an attribute our culture has been inclined to associate more with mothers. Hosea 11 is one of many passages in the Bible in which feelings and activities that many modern people tend to attribute to women are attributed to God.

## God and Other Nations (Isaiah 10 and 19)

Hosea's theology of history was confined to the history of Israel, and there are no oracles concerning foreign nations. Other nations are alluded to, but primarily as powers that Israel depended upon to compensate for its own weakness (e.g., 5:13 and 7:8-11). However, there are a few references to foreign nations as instruments of God's judgment against Israel (7:16; 9:3, 6; 10:6; 11:5). In other books of the prophets there are extended oracles and groups of oracles concerning foreign nations. We have chosen just two of these to include in the present discussion. One of them concerns God's judgment against a foreign nation, and the second concerns God's redemption of foreign nations. The texts are Isa 10:5-21 and Isa 19:16-25.

"Woe Assyria, the rod of my anger, the staff of my fury!" Thus begins Isaiah's famous oracle. It is a literary masterpiece and a brilliant theological statement. Heretofore in this book we have paid little attention to the literary features of the passages. However, the literary form of the present text is so

elegant and contributes so to the discernment of its message
that it deserves comment. In vv 5 and 6 God declares that
Assyria is the instrument of his punishment of a godless nation
(Israel is to be understood). V 7 declares that Assyria's purpose
in this enterprise is quite different from God's. It is not to
punish, but to destroy. Vv 8-11 quote the vainglorious boasting
of the Assyrian conqueror. V 12, which stands at the center of
the oracle, is in prose. It affirms the twofold purpose of God,
first to punish Mount Zion and Jerusalem, and then to punish
Assyria. Vv 13-14 resume the poetic development of the oracle;
they return to the theme of Assyria's pride, shown in the
conquest of nations. V 15 asks the question whether an axe can
vaunt itself above its wielder. Finally, vv 16-19 describe the
devastation which God will bring upon Assyria. The seven
segments of the oracle contain, respectively, the following
number of poetic lines (in Hebrew): 3, 2, 6 (brief prose
interlude), 6, 2, and 6. The form is chiastic. The prose
statement of the twofold purpose of God at the center of the
composition is preceded and followed by the two six-line
exhibitions of the pride of Assyria. These in turn are flanked by
two-line references to the contradiction between Assyria's
purpose and God's. Then, on the outside of this structure, at
the beginning and end of the oracle, are two announcements of
God's wrath. The first is against Israel and the second against
Assyria. The second is twice as long as the first, befitting the
climactic section of the composition. If the reader will mark the
sections of the poem with penciled brackets in the margins of a
Bible in the way I have indicated, this finely articulated form
will become evident. The seven elements are vv 5-6, 7, 8-11, 12,
13-14, 15, and 16-19.

Clearly, Isaiah believed God was the Lord of Assyria as well
as Israel. Furthermore, his oracle implies that God was Lord of
all the nations of the earth. This point becomes explicit when we
read the other oracles concerning foreign nations in the Book of
Isaiah (chaps. 13–23). In Isaiah's theological perspective the
conquest of Israel by Assyria constituted a just punishment by

God for Israel's godlessness. The specific content of her wickedness is not spelled out in the present text, but it is expounded by Isaiah in his other oracles. The point here is that God's justice toward the nation is executed in the interactions of nations. In this case the judgment of God is executed by a nation whose own understanding of history is quite different from Isaiah's. It is thus the unknowing instrument of God's righteousness. The prophet, viewing international affairs in the perspective of faith, discerns the justice of God at work there. The participants in these affairs may not see this dimension at all.

The next assertion is that Assyria, the mighty conqueror, will eventually receive the same punishment for its pround defiance of God as it had mediated to Israel. God is no respecter of nations. The means of Assyria's punishment would be the same as Israel's, namely, conquest by another nation. To this extent the judgment of God is observed within the processes of history. Secular historians viewing the same events might discern a causal coherence in the interactions of nations, but they would not attribute it to the working of a transcendent, divine justice. The prophet, viewing this interaction through the eyes of faith, sees within it the providence of God.

Before asking whether this prophetic perception can illuminate our own understanding of history, we will turn to a different sort of oracle concerning non-Israelite nations. Most of the oracles on foreign nations in the OT pronounce God's judgment against arrogance and oppression, and, like Isa 10:5-21, envision the working out of God's justice through the conflicts of nations and the rise and fall of rulers. Some of them manifest an internationalist perspective that transcends national zeal and sectarian prejudice. The best example of this kind of oracle is Amos 1–2. Many others exhibit Israelite nationalism, e.g., Ezek 25:1-7. A few prophetic writers looked beyond the horizon of their own national interests and imagined the operation of a creative providence among the nations. The most notable of these was the author of Isaiah

40–55, whose constructive vision was truly worldwide. Another was the anonymous writer of the brief but remarkable word in Isa 19:23-25. This text stands in the midst of a series of oracles of judgment against Egypt (chaps. 19–20). The conviction and sentiment expressed in this prophecy are astonishing to find in any ancient writing. "In that day Israel will be the third with Egypt and Assyria, a blessing in the midst of the earth, whom the Lord of Hosts has blessed, saying, 'Blessed be Egypt my people, and Assyria the work of my hands, and Israel my heritage'" (vv 24-25). Assyria and Egypt were the upper and lower millstones between which Israel was ground throughout most of her history. For an Israelite prophet to compose these lines required extraordinary cultural transcendence. The passage contains no statement of the theological ground for the writer's prophecy. However, it must have been rooted in faith in the universal sovereignty of God and the will of God to create a harmonious community of nations in the world. The oracle preceding this one, which could be from the same writer, prophesies the conversion of the Egyptians to the worship of Yahweh, and thus suggests that a common devotion to the one Lord would provide the bond uniting the peoples into a single community.

Can these ancient texts have any meaning for us, other than as sources for the history of ideas? This is a difficult question. The dream of international harmony expressed in Isa 19:23-25 is an ideal that has persisted through the centuries and has had widespread currency in our time. However, the actualities of history, esp. the twentieth century, make it appear little more than an ideal. Nevertheless, the spirit that animates this ideal can affect attitudes and behavior powerfully, esp. among small groups, but also among nations. The prophetic conviction that tyrannical, rapacious powers will eventually fall is still credible today. We know that tyranny and oppression, among nations, groups, and individuals, often last a long time, and that there is seldom a perfect correlation between what is deserved and what is received. The OT prophets knew these things, too, but they were not deterred by this knowledge from proclaiming the righteousness of God.

## The Righteous Ruler and the New Covenant
## (Isaiah 11 and Jeremiah 31)

The prophetic oracles concerning foreign nations deal with what we might call the gross justice of God as it is implemented through the interactions of nations within the historical process. This is a gross rather than a precise justice because of the freedom that human beings have to shape their destiny, and because of the host of fortuitous circumstances affecting the course of history. Many righteous acts go unrewarded and many evil acts unpunished. Many noble efforts in behalf of human rights are thwarted, while many unjust social systems persist for generations. In these and other ways, justice is frustrated. The fulfillment of the righteous purposes of God among the nations, as these are conceived in prophetic theology, remains incomplete from generation to generation. Consequently, the prophetic interpretation of history includes the promise of a future fulfillment of the righteousness of God. This promise takes many forms. Jeremiah 33 (which seems unlikely to have been written by Jeremiah himself) prophesies the restoration of the Judean monarchy in the land of Canaan. The great blueprint for the future people of God in Ezekiel 40–48 describes a theocratic government and a society controlled by priests, in place of the traditional monarchy. Other prophetic texts contain a more ecumenical vision of the future. We have already referred to one of these, Isa 19:23-25. The greatest of them all is Isaiah 40–55, which prophesies the unfolding of God's purpose for the nations in a single world empire, ruled in righteousness by God's anointed leader and taught by the prophetic servants of the Lord (45:1-25 and 49:1-13, et al.). A full exposition of the prophetic teaching concerning the righteousness of God would have to take account of these and other texts. Such an exposition is beyond the scope of this book, but our discussion would be deficient if it omitted all consideration of a motif we have not yet mentioned. It has to do with the fulfillment of God's righteous purpose through the mediation of righteous people.

The achievement of justice and the other values that enhance life in community requires righteous rulers and righteous people. Isa 11:1-9 presents a picture of the righteous ruler who promotes the good of his people, and Jer 31:31-34 describes a good people. These two texts have no literary relationship to one another and are the work of different writers. The first is thought by many biblical scholars to be the work of the eighth-century Isaiah. However, some regard it as the work of an anonymous writer of a later time, perhaps during the Exile in the sixth century. The text from Jeremiah is attributed by most commentators to Jeremiah himself; however, it has much in common with the prose traditions of the Book of Jeremiah, which are primarily the work of the prophet's followers. Therefore it too may be from an anonymous exilic hand. I have chosen these two passages with which to conclude the present chapter, not because of any literary or historical relation between them, but because they express so well the two elements of prophetic thought just stated, viz., that the achievement of justice in society requires righteous rulers and righteous people.

Isa 11:1-9, a familiar messianic passage, is one of several passages concerning the Israelite king. The royal office was considered sacred in ancient Israel, and a special ritual of anointing consecrated the king for the service of God. Monarchy is almost always hereditary and in ancient Judah the hereditary principle became firmly established in the dynasty of David. The Davidic claim to sole legitimacy was supported by a tradition of divine election, which was expressed in the oracle of Nathan in 2 Samuel 7. This tradition was celebrated in Judean worship (Psalm 89), and it helped to secure the Davidic line in the Kingdom of Judah until the destruction of Jerusalem in 586 B.C. (e.g., 1 Kgs 8:16-19).

Isaiah 11 may reflect the influence of the royal liturgies that were celebrated in the temple of Jerusalem. The substance of these liturgies may be traced in the royal psalms, which probably arose in this setting (Ps 2, 18, 20, 21, 45, 72, 89, 101, 110, 132, 144). There is no evidence in the book that Isaiah challenged the dynastic principle itself or the tradition of God's election of the line of David. However, he was severely critical of the contemporary Judean king, Ahaz, for his conduct of national affairs (chaps. 7 and 8), and it is against the background of this criticism that we may view the portrait of the ideal Davidic ruler in chap. 11. It should be read together with the companion oracle 9:1-7, which describes a future deliverance of the people of God from oppression, the renewal of sovereignty for the Davidic king, and the establishment of peace. All this would take place through the power of God (v 7). The oracle in chap. 11 deals with the characteristics of the future king and the manner of his rule. Thus it describes the internal qualities of government by the vicegerent of God, whereas chap. 9 depicts the outward manifestations of the establishment of sovereignty by the anointed Davidic king (the "Messiah").

The oracle in 11:1-9 is framed as the promise of a future king, and we may accept it as a genuine prophecy in this sense. Therefore it is legitimate for interpreters of the Bible to ask whether and in what way this prophecy was fulfilled. Christians, beginning at least as early as Paul (Rom 15:12), have regarded Jesus Christ as the fulfillment, although they acknowledge that the promised age of peace and harmony has not yet been realized. Jews regard both the promise of an age of peace and promise of a messianic ruler as unfulfilled.

This oracle is a messianic prophecy, but it is also a model of the ideal ruler, and as such can serve as a guide and stimulus to rulers in the present age, even though no actual ruler could achieve that standard perfectly and permanently. Self-interest and finitude inevitably affect every government, and the conflicting demands of the people who are governed preclude the achievement of perfect justice or permanent harmony.

Nevertheless, rulers sharing the religious convictions of an Isaiah can learn from this model and rule more justly as a consequence.

In this oracle, the foundation of just rule is faith in God. It is the knowledge and fear of Yahweh from which the other qualities flow (11:2). This faith is not perfunctory or peripheral—something required traditionally by the office—but the central reality of the ruler's life. He delights in it! (v 3). The Spirit of God is manifested first of all in the protection of the rights of the weak and the poor and in the restraint of evil (v 4). However, this justice is not achieved through the ordinary use of violence, or the threat of violence, but by the intrinsic authority of the king's word. For such authority to be truly operative it requires the consent of the governed. This means there must be a people whose life and values are rooted in faith in God and who are willing to be subjects of a ruler whose administration is built upon this foundation.

The famous new-covenant text in Jer 31:31-34 is the prophecy of a future event, and it bears many similarities to Isa 11:1-9. It may be regarded by Christian interpreters as having been fulfilled in the creation of the Christian community through the life, death, and resurrection of Jesus of Nazareth. It may also function as a model of covenantal obedience in any age, quite apart from its association with the Christian proclamation. The obedience to God that characterizes the people of the New Covenant arises from personal knowledge of God, i.e., from faith, and fulfillment of covenantal law is achieved, not by external constraint, but by willing compliance arising out of the disposition of the heart. Here is a prophetic promise of forgiveness of iniquity offered by God, which is the only effective way to break the power of guilt. The statement that there will be no need for religious instruction, for everyone will already have attained the knowledge of God (v 34), points forward to the ultimate fulfillment of the people's existence in faith. It is not a simple description of any actual human community, though the promise of the oracle was partially fulfilled in the life of the Jewish community in the generations following Jeremiah's pronouncement. Although the promise contains the statement of an ideal that eludes total achievement by any people in history, it is an ideal that can be partially achieved in a community of faith. In this sense the oracle can serve as a model for existing religious communities as well as a promise of the future fulfillment of the purposes of God.

The righteousness of God is manifested in the fulfillment of creation. It is positive, life-supporting, enabling, nurturing, disciplining, and caring. It is not punitive or destructive. It elicits righteousness from the creatures and thus fulfills itself and them. This positive goal of the activity of God is suggested eloquently in the two prophecies from the books of Isaiah and Jeremiah.

# V. "WHO IS LIKE GOD?"

Each of the passages we have discussed expresses or presupposes an understanding of God and God's relationship to the world, and so they might well have been included in the present chapter. By the same token, the two texts to be studied here (Isaiah 40 and Ezekiel 34) could have been treated appropriately in the preceding chapter, for they speak about God's activity as the righteous Lord of creation. We will consider them separately in order to focus attention upon the question of the nature of God. The first is the introductory poem to the great work of the Second Isaiah, and the second is Ezekiel's prophecy of the Good Shepherd. Both come from the exilic period.

No abstract doctrine of God is stated in the OT. There is no systematic or philosophical discussion of the nature or attributes of God and no argument for the existence of God against those who might question it. There was no secular atheism among the peoples of the ancient world, and many of the questions that arise in modern minds concerning the existence of and nature of God did not occur to ancient minds. The existence of invisible, superhuman, personal powers and their active involvement in the human environment were taken for granted by everyone. These were the immemorial assumptions that permeated people's perception of the world and their thoughts and feelings about their relation to it. Divine power and will were at work everywhere, and everything depended upon them. All of life, both corporate and individual, was lived in awareness of such forces and was punctuated by ritual acts, again both corporate and individual, aimed at attaining fuller comprehension and control of these powers and responding more appropriately to them. The most religious people in modern Western society would appear to be irreligious if compared with ordinary people in the biblical world. The imaginations of ancient people were filled with gods, spirits, and demons, and their lives were regulated at every turn by rituals predicated upon the demands, promises, or threats of these beings. Atheism for most ancient people was simply inconceivable, and so was life without regular worship of the gods.

Throughout the history of ancient Israel there was a profound struggle between the religions of the environing peoples and Israel's faith in Yahweh. Both involved an understanding of reality in which the Divine played a central part. The difference lay in their conceptions of the Divine. One was polytheistic and involved the deification of powers in nature (earth, sky, rain, sun, sea, etc.). It also involved an interpretation of the processes of nature according to the analogy of animal procreation. Things came to be and were renewed in the world as a result of the sexual mating of gods and goddesses, and much of the ritual practice of religion was intended to support this regeneration and respond to it suitably. Individual deities were imagined in human or animal form and were symbolized accordingly. The processes of nature and the structures of society were described in myths, and these provided the intellectual background for the performance of ritual and were sometimes dramatized in the rituals themselves. Offerings to the gods were often magical, in the sense that they were meant to coerce or purchase the favor and intervention of the gods, and the omission of offerings and other ritual acts from the routine of human life would place the whole human enterprise in jeopardy. Good and ill fortune were determined, battles were won and lost, kings rose and fell, crops flourished or failed, people lived and died by the will of the gods. Sometimes the gods acted arbitrarily, but sometimes they acted in response to human behavior, including the performance or omission of worship. Disease and health were controlled by the gods, although disease was often interpreted as possession by demonic powers. Healing, therefore, was sought through propitiation of the gods or exorcism of the demons. The cycle of the seasons was celebrated, and the fertility of crops and flocks was supported by rituals designed to assure the favor of the gods and assist in the regulation of the natural processes. Kings ruled by the will of the gods, and kingship itself was established on the earth as a mirror of divine rule. The rituals that accompanied the birth and enthronement of kings and the major events of their reigns were profoundly religious matters. In these and many other ways, the life of ancient people was founded upon and permeated by an intense and active polytheism.

Israelite Yahwism contended with this understanding and way of life throughout its history. We can obtain a rough idea of this struggle from the OT. However, the account is incomplete and biased for it oversimplifies the picture of the rival religion as well as the account of the conflict between the two faiths. As a result we cannot determine accurately who in Israel at various stages in its history shared the faith expressed in the OT itself. The OT is the final literary product of the history of Yahwism, and through it we receive fragmentary glimpses of its earlier developments, but we do not know with certainty what the persons mentioned in the OT story believed or exactly how they practiced their religion, except for the prophets, whose own writings are incorporated in the canonical OT. We can be certain only about the faith of the writers of the OT, and most of them are anonymous. We can only speculate about the faith of

oracles from the preexilic period are short, staccato, slashing, and critical, and place the speaker in confrontation with the audience. In contrast, the poems of Second Isaiah "speak to the heart" (v 2) of the hearer, appealing and encouraging, and placing the speaker in sympathetic relation to the audience. This requires repetition and persuasion, the creation of a mood, the stirring of feelings. This poem is not so much a text to be used as the starting point of a sermon, it is a sermon. Yet, how much more stirring and memorable than the discursive prose sermons in the Book of Jeremiah!

The poem is positive from beginning to end. It opens with an admonition to the messengers of God to comfort his people, and it ends with the affirmation that those who wait upon, or trust in, the Lord will be sustained. Thus the mood of this opening section conforms entirely to that of the joyful, exuberant closing passage, Isaiah 55, which we discussed earlier. Every line of the poem merits careful reflection. However, we will make only a few comments upon some of the salient features.

The initial injunction to comfort the people of God and declare his pardon for all their iniquities is followed immediately by another command to prepare the way of God in the wilderness, so that his glory may be beheld by all flesh (vv 3-5). Thus, the word of comfort is reinforced by the assurance of the imminent coming of God. Then this second word gives way to the third, in which the transience of all humanity is contrasted with the permanence of the word of God (vv 6-8). Thus, the three opening themes of the work are, first, comfort and forgiveness, second, the impending appearance of God's glory as the sign of his presence, and third, the everlasting reliability of God's word amidst an evanescent humanity. In sum, God's comfort, God's glory, God's word.

The next section of the chapter (vv 9-17) has three segments parallel in content to the three we have just considered. The first affirms that God is coming, with his reward and recompense before him, to be the shepherd of the flock (vv

9-11). The second speaks about who God is (vv 12-14), and the third contrasts the insignificance of the nations with the grandeur of God (vv 15-17).

The third section of the poem (vv 18-31) has two principal segments. In the first, which opens with the question, "To whom then would you liken God?" elaborates upon the theme introduced in the second division about the absurdity and futility of idols (vv 18-24). This segment closes by asserting that God brings the rulers of the earth to nothing, thus echoing the concluding comment in the second division of the poem (vv 23-24, cf. v 15). The final segment of the third division, which concludes the entire poem, brings us back to the opening theme, viz., the word of comfort and assurance to the people of God. It asks, "Why do you say, O Jacob, and speak, O Israel, 'My way is hid from the Lord . . . ?'" (v 27) and goes on to reply to this question. The message is addressed to discouraged Israelites who have given up on God. Here the practical goal of the proclamation is reached, and the reason for the repeated contrast between human finitude and divine transcendence becomes clear. The discouraged Israelites are to take heart, place their confidence in the unsearchable power of God, and allow themselves to be revived and strengthened in their way (vv 27-31). "They who wait upon the Lord . . . shall walk and not faint." This is the goal of the prophecy.

The fall of the Kingdom of Judah, the destruction of Jerusalem, and the exile of the nation's leaders appeared to many to demonstrate the ineffectiveness of Yahweh, the God of Israel, and caused them to turn to the worship of other gods, esp. the gods of the conquering Babylonians (Jer 44:15-30). Isaiah 40–55 responds to the despair underlying this behavior and the inadequacy of the idolatries to which the people have turned. The prophet's treatment of the theme of idolatry is introduced only briefly in chap. 40 and is expanded in subsequent poems. In contrast to the various idolatries, which deify objects and forces within nature, the conception of God presented by Second Isaiah places the entire natural order within the comprehension and power of God. This picture of Yahweh as sovereign creator of all things makes explicit an element in Israel's faith that is only implicit in some other OT writings. Genesis 1, the Book of Job, and some of the Psalms, are OT texts that definitely express this concept, and they may be roughly contemporary with Second Isaiah. Here in Isaiah 40 the implications of the prophetic faith in one God are made evident. There is but one God, and this God is both sustainer of Israel and creator of the heavens and the earth.

The understanding of God as creator of the natural order is linked with that of God as sovereign over the historical order. Nations are subject to this sovereignty, just as the stars are. It manifests itself in both the humbling of the mighty (v 23) and the empowering of the weary (vv 29-31). Creation and providence are thus united in the activity of the one God. Although the prophet expressed this faith in a new way, he insisted that he was proclaiming to Israel what they had been told from the beginning, what indeed should have been understood from the foundations of the earth (v 21). Here and elsewhere Second Isaiah shows how the new message he is proclaiming is rooted in the old witness of Israel's faith.

The coming revelation of God's glory, which is announced at the beginning of the poem, is an event described only symbolically in chap. 40, in the image of the leveling out of valleys and hills to prepare a processional highway for the appearance of God (v 4). In subsequent chaps. this event is described in concrete historical terms. Indeed, the entire collection of Second Isaiah's poems is an elaboration of this theme. The whole community of nations will be involved in this vast historical development. It will include the conquest of Babylon by Cyrus and the creation of a great world empire (cf., e.g., chap. 45). It will also involve the dissemination of God's *torah* and the establishment of God's justice (42:4) by Israel, the servant of Yahweh. And it will include the release of exiled Israelite captives and the restoration of the city of Jerusalem as the focal point of the witness to God and his saving purpose (e.g., 40:9; 48:20; 49:8-18). Thus, although the major themes of the work are stated in chap. 40, it is only an introduction to the rich exposition in chaps. 41–55.

The understanding of God expressed in Isaiah 40 is clear and coherent. However, in the actual experience of human beings, in both ancient and modern times, this faith is not held by everyone, nor is it easily attained. The prophet himself was aware of this, for he observed that witnesses of God come to understand the God whom they proclaim in the very process of bearing witness (43:10 and 50:4). The teacher learns by teaching, and the messengers of God come to full understanding by proclaiming the word to others. The role of the witnesses, who form an ever-widening circle from Jerusalem to the ends of the earth, is indicated already in the introductory poem (vv 3, 6), and it occupies a central place in the subsequent chapters.

The message of Isaiah 40–55 was the announcement of a drama of salvation, which the prophet believed to be unfolding in his own time, and it was a summons to his fellow Israelites to play their proper part in this drama. Before discussing the outcome of this proclamation and its possible relevance to the life of a modern reader, let us turn to Ezekiel 34.

### The Good Shepherd (Ezekiel 34)

Ezekiel 34 is an allegory of the history of Israel under the monarchy, and a prophecy of the future restoration of the nation. There are many historical allusions that we would have to probe in a thorough exegesis. However, we are only considering it here because of what it says about God, and so we will not follow the other exegetical paths suggested in the text.

Earlier we examined several other passages from the Book of Ezekiel that represent God as the punitive judge of idolators in Jerusalem (8:16, 9:11) and as the guarantor of a strict, retributive justice in the lives of individual persons (chap. 18). It comes as something of a surprise, therefore, to see the

wrathful executioner and impersonal judge displaced by a
shepherd eager to rescue, protect, and provision his flock. The
metaphor of the shepherd implies many of the qualities
suggested by the metaphors of husband and parent in Hosea 2
and 11. The shepherd-image is less satisfactory than the images
drawn from family relationships, since human beings are
symbolized much more adequately as children or brides than as
sheep. Nevertheless, from the side of the shepherd/husband/
parent there are common dimensions of commitment and
affection that are connoted by all of these metaphors. It is
noteworthy that the image of God as the Good Shepherd,
which received its classic formulation in Ezekiel 34, became one
of the most popular images in later Jewish and Christian piety
and iconography.

Ezekiel's allegory of the shepherds and the Good Shepherd
says much about his understanding of God and his understanding of the function of kingship. For him, kings are clearly meant
to be servants of God and God's people, in contrast to what the
kings of Israel had made of the institution. Several interesting
points emerge in his treatment of God as the Good Shepherd.
Perhaps the most important is the statement that God actively
searches for the lost sheep, rescuing, gathering, and feeding
them. This is not a dispassionate judge, but an impassioned
savior. The goal of God's activity in the lives of people is to seek
the lost, gather the strayed, heal the crippled, and empower the
weak. This is also the proper goal of the servants of God,
according to Ezekiel.

The shepherd "watches over" the strong as well as the weak
(v 16, reading *Smr* with the Greek, Syriac, and Vulgate, and
RSV, CBAT, JB, and NEB). It would make little sense to
"destroy" them (*Smd,* MT), even though the shepherd may
have to judge some of them (vv 17-22). God shepherds the
entire flock.

In Ezekiel's prophecy the Davidic monarchy is to be
reestablished in Israel (vv 23, 24), and his conception of that
future life is conservative, in the sense that it projects the

preexilic form of the nation. Second Isaiah does not do this with respect to the Davidic monarchy, but instead envisions Israel's role as that of prophet and teacher within a world empire ruled by a non-Israelite king. What actually happened in the postexilic era was much closer to Second Isaiah's vision than to Ezekiel's. However, the principal emphasis of Ezekiel 34 is not upon the restoration of the Davidic monarchy. This event is only one aspect of the unfolding purpose of God. The ultimate goal of the drama is to bring people to the knowledge of God. The making of a new covenant, the provision of natural blessings, the freeing of slaves, the establishment of peace and security, all serve one purpose: "And they shall know that I, the Lord their God, am with them, and that they, the house of Israel, are my people, says the Lord God" (v 31). Living in the knowledge of God is the goal of the entire process of human history and divine providence.

We return now to the questions we asked above concerning the outcome of the promises made in Isaiah 40 and Ezekiel 34 and their meaning for modern readers.

Both passages anticipate events that are to take place at some time in the future, when God will be present, will act decisively, and will be acknowledged as God. Were these anticipations actualized, and if so, in what way? If not, are they still to be realized, or were the prophets wrong? In either case, what meaning can their prophecies have for modern readers?

Clearly, when Second Isaiah speaks about God's appearing in glory (40:5), he is not speaking of an appearance visible to eyes of flesh, even though he asserts that "all flesh" shall behold the appearance. The God who "measured the waters in the hollow of his hand" (v 12) is not visible to human eyes in any circumstances. The glory of God, whose manifestation the writer prophesies, can be seen only with eyes of faith. It is the same glory that "filled the whole earth" according to the First Isaiah's inaugural vision (6:3). Just as the glory which fills the whole earth was already visible in Isaiah's time to those who had eyes to see, so the glory which Second Isaiah prophesied would be manifest only to those who had faith. However, in that event all humanity would have been brought to faith, so all would behold the glory. The eyes of faith and the eyes of unfaith observe exactly the same phenomena, but the one regards them as manifestations of God's power and wisdom, while the other sees only what they appear to be.

If the future appearance of God in glory anticipated in Isaiah 40 is not essentially different from the presence of God which could be known in the present, then we would not have to posit "a new heaven and a new earth" as the precondition of fulfillment. Both Isaiah 40 and Ezekiel 34 seem to be speaking about the not-too-distant future. Indeed, the events heralded by Second Isaiah are already beginning to take place in his own time. In chap. 34 Ezekiel is anticipating a time somewhat farther into the future, though not necessarily more than a few generations. His hope of a restoration of the Israelite nation might reasonably have been expected to be fulfilled in that length of time. The next question, then, is whether the expectations of these two writers were actually realized in subsequent years.

Specific aspects of the two prophecies were not fulfilled. The Davidic dynasty was not restored to power as Ezekiel had expected, and the creation of a unified world empire with Jerusalem as the spiritual center was not achieved. However, some of the hopes of our two writers were fulfilled significantly. Babylon was conquered by Cyrus, who did establish a more just and humane policy toward subject peoples. Jewish exiles were permitted to return to their homeland. Jerusalem was rebuilt, and the temple of Yahweh reestablished. New forms of social organization, worship, and education were developed among Jewish communities. The people of the covenant increased enormously in numbers, and they became one of the most creative peoples of the ancient world. The institution of the synagogue took form in the postexilic era, and it has persisted to the present day as a fundamental institution of Judaism. The Hebrew Bible was given its canonical form in those centuries also, and ultimately became the Holy Scriptures for millions of Jews and Christians. These are the principal ways in which the glory of God appeared to those who had eyes to see.

> • As we have observed many times before, the OT writers were not concerned to formulate general truths about God or humanity, but spoke primarily about their own times and people and the ways of God as they perceived them in Israel's experience. Therefore, many of the biblical texts do not lend themselves simply to religious instruction for modern readers, and it is difficult to move directly from Isaiah 40 and Ezekiel 34 to our own situation. They are concerned, after all, with the conditions and prospects of Israel in the sixth century B.C. One of our responsibilities as interpreters of the Bible is to acknowledge the time-bound features of these texts and not try to force them to speak to us in ways they were not meant to do. Nevertheless, there are elements in them which can illuminate our understanding of God.

God is the savior in Isaiah 40 and Ezekiel 34. This is the understanding of God that dominates the story of Israel in the Pentateuch and the Psalms, and it reappears again and again in the Prophets. Christians are often unaware of this, or disregard it. It is common for Christians to exalt the NT at the expense of the OT, by contrasting the NT message of salvation with "the OT message of judgment." However, this is an inadequate interpretation of the Bible. There is judgment in both testaments, but both are founded on faith in God as creator and redeemer. The story of Israel is a story of salvation. The prophecy of salvation in Isaiah 40 and Ezekiel 34 is a renewal of God's promise to Abraham (Genesis 12) and to Moses (Exodus 3), and it is the message that unites the OT, as well as the NT.

The primary relevance of these two texts (and the others we have discussed) for modern readers lies in this understanding of God as creator and savior. The basic meaning of these texts was what they said to Judean exiles 2500 years ago about their situation, their prospects, and their faith. Their meaning for us is twofold. We can see the witness of faith in God as it worked in ancient Israel, and we can reaffirm that faith ourselves. The fruits of God's word are always appropriate to the time in which it is spoken, and they may not be the same in every age. And yet, it is the same God whose word is spoken. Knowledge of the prophets' faith in God, which found expression in their writings but which even more undergirded them, is the principal meaning of these texts for us.

# AIDS FOR THE INTERPRETER

## Translation

Interpreters without Hebrew should make use of all the help available in recent English translations to determine the meaning of the text. Translations by individuals are less authoritative than the ones listed here, all of which are by qualified teams. Avoid *The Living Bible,* which is not a translation and cannot be trusted to represent the Bible's meaning. Most of the versions listed are evaluated in detail in Lloyd Bailey, ed., *The Word of God* (Atlanta: John Knox Press, 1982). Use them all.

*The Complete Bible, An American Translation.* Chicago: University of Chicago Press, 1939.

*Good News Bible, Today's English Version.* New York: American Bible Society, 1976.

*The Holy Bible, New International Version.* Grand Rapids: Zondervan Bible Publishers, 1978.

*The Jerusalem Bible.* New York: Doubleday & Co., 1966.

*The New American Bible.* New York: P. J. Kenedy & Sons, 1970.

*New American Standard Bible.* La Habra, Calif.: Lockman Foundation, 1963.

*The New English Bible with the Apocrypha,* Oxford Study Edition. New York: Oxford University Press, 1976.

*The New Oxford Annotated Bible with the Apocrypha, Revised Standard Version.* New York: Oxford University Press, 1973.

*A New Translation of the Holy Scriptures According to the Masoretic Text (New Jewish Version).* Philadelphia: Jewish Publication Society of America, 1962, 1978.

Be sure to buy the annotated editions of the RSV, NEB, and JB.

## Reference and Commentary

A complete concordance is essential. Those of Robert Young *(Analytical Concordance to the Bible)* and James Strong *(Exhaustive Concordance of the Bible)* are based on the King James Version. However, they provide access to the Hebrew and Greek words behind the English. They will be superseded by C. Morrison, *An Analytical Concordance to the RSV.* The NT section was published in 1979, and the OT section is in preparation.

*The Interpreter's Dictionary of the Bible* (5 vols. Nashville: Abingdon Press, 1962, 1976) is invaluable.

The treatments of the prophets in *The Interpreter's Bible,* vols. 5 and 6 (Nashville: Abingdon Press, 1956) are generally good and often excellent. The Old Testament Library (Philadelphia: The Westminster Press) is solid, too: Otto Kaiser, *Isaiah 1–12* (1972), *Isaiah 13–39* (1974); Claus Westermann, *Isaiah 40–66* (1969); Walter Eichrodt, *Ezekiel* (1970); James L. Mays, *Hosea* (1969), *Amos* (1969), *Micah* (1976). The *New International Commentary on the Old Testament* (Grand Rapids: Eerdmans Publishing Co.) has good volumes so far by Leslie C. Allen on *Joel, Obadiah, Jonah, Micah* (1976); and by J. A. Thompson on *Jeremiah* (1980). The commentaries in the series Hermeneia (Philadelphia: Fortress Press) are thorough and technical: Hans Walter Wolff, *Hosea* (1974), *Joel and Amos* (1977); Walter Zimmerli, *Ezekiel* (vol. 1, 1978, vol. 2 in preparation).

## Interpretation

There are not many profound works in English on the theology of the Prophets. Gerhard von Rad, *The Message of the Prophets* (New York: Harper & Row, 1962, 1975; this is part of vol. 2 of his *Old Testament Theology*) is perhaps the best in print. Martin Buber, *The Prophetic Faith* (New York: The Macmillan Co., 1949) is excellent, but out of print. Look for a used copy. Abraham Herschel, *The Prophets* (New York: Harper & Row, 1962) is valuable, too.

The best, thorough book on the whole phenomenon of prophecy is Johannes Lindblom, *Prophecy in Ancient Israel* (Oxford: Basil Blackwell, 1962).

Good books on individual prophetic books are: William L. Holladay, *Isaiah: Scroll of a Prophetic Heritage* (Grand Rapids: Eerdmans Publishing Co., 1978), and Hans Walter Wolff, *Micah the Prophet* (Philadelphia: Fortress Press, 1981).

The series of paperbacks for preachers (and others), Knox Preaching Guides (Atlanta: John Knox Press), emphasizes the meaning of the biblical books for today. All the Prophets will be treated, beginning with *Amos and Hosea* (1981), by James M. Ward.

Another paperback series, Proclamation Commentaries (Philadelphia: Fortress Press) is also useful, though it confines itself largely to the original meaning of the text. Volumes available so far on the Prophets are: Bernhard W. Anderson, *The Eighth Century Prophets* (1978), James L. Mays, *Ezekiel, Second Isaiah* (1978), and Elizabeth Achtemeier, *Deuteronomy, Jeremiah* (1978).